Affectionally Dad

Affectionately, Dad

Letters to Vernon, 1922-1938

by
William M. Crook

edited by
Roger H. Crook

BROADMAN PRESS
Nashville, Tennessee

Dewey Decimal Classification: 306.8
Subject Headings: FATHERS//PARENT AND CHILD
Library of Congress Catalog Card Number: 80-67461
Printed in the United States of America

INTRODUCTION

William Murphy Crook was born October 6, 1885, at Cameron, North Carolina. He was the younger of two children, both boys, born to Alexander Turner Crook and Priscilla Anne Rogers Crook. Alexander, at the time of his marriage to Priscilla, had two children, Laura and Jimmy, by his first wife who had died. Until the time of his death, Alexander Crook operated a farm in Moore County, North Carolina, near Cameron.

William (or "Will") Crook was born with a hereditary physical condition which only in recent years has been identified as the Marfan Syndrome. Among other characteristics, the syndrome involved serious difficulties of the heart and eyes. Though not totally blind, Will had a severe visual handicap. In the fall of 1896, therefore, just before he reached the age of eleven, he entered the North Carolina State School for the Blind in Raleigh.

Will attended the School for the Blind until he was graduated from high school, and then taught there for two years, 1903-1905. During the next twelve years he taught in the public schools in several communities in North Carolina: Roxobel, Star, Bynum, and Harrisburg. In 1917 he was employed as an officer and teacher at the Jackson Training School, Concord, North Carolina, where he remained until his death on January 21, 1939.

On August 27, 1907, Will was married to Mary Blanche Hawley, a teacher who had lived on a farm at Swan Station, near Jonesboro, not far from Will's home. He and Blanche had four sons. Vernon Baldwin, the recipient of these letters, was born March 25, 1909. William Elroy was born September 23, 1911. Harold Lamar was born October 10, 1914. And

Roger Hawley was born October 5, 1921.

Two of Will Crook's sons, Vernon and Harold, inherited the Marfan Syndrome from their father. Like him, they were so severely handicapped visually that they needed help and treatment not available to them in the public schools. Like him, therefore, they attended the State School for the Blind. Vernon entered the seventh grade there, and remained there until he was graduated from high school. Harold was there for a year and a half, and then returned to the public school at Harrisburg.

In September 1922, Blanche took thirteen-year-old Vernon to begin his education at the School for the Blind. Within a few days after their departure, and before Blanche had returned home, Will wrote his first letter to his son. From that time on Vernon was to spend only his summer vacations with his parents. Every week either Will or Blanche, and sometimes both of them, wrote to him. That correspondence continued throughout those years in Raleigh, then the college years at the University of North Carolina in Chapel Hill, and afterward while Vernon was working in Chapel Hill.

For reasons which even he does not now know, Vernon saved all of the letters from his parents. His mother's letters were chatty, full of news, replete with the trivia of day-by-day living. His father's letters, as the reader will learn, were sometimes philosophic, often humorous, occasionally didactic, always reflective. They reveal not only family relationships and concerns but also the social and economic situation of a Southern white, middle-class family of the twenties and thirties. And they reveal a religious faith that was natural and unaffected.

Throughout the time of the writing of these letters, Will Crook was employed at the Jackson Training School, a state reform school for boys. Many neighbors referred to in these letters were fellow employees there. As an "officer" at the Training School Will was assigned to one of the cottages in which the youthful offenders were housed. There were approximately thirty boys to each cottage. For each cottage there was a matron who was responsible for household management.

And for each there were two officers who alternated cottage duty weekly. When an officer was on duty, he got the boys up in time for breakfast, around 6:00 AM, and had a responsibility for them until he put them to bed at 8:00 PM. The week, it should be noted, was a full seven days! When an officer was off duty, his responsibilities began at breakfast and ended with the evening meal. During the day, some officers worked with boys in the fields or in one of the shops (printing, carpentry, shoe repair, etc.). Others taught in the classroom. During his entire twenty-two years at the school, Crook taught the sixth grade. In addition to these assigned duties, Crook, a devout Christian, taught a Sunday School class at the school. He also established and operated a lending library for the boys. His letters to Vernon are full of references to his work in all of these areas.

Crook's obituary in the periodical published by the Jackson Training School was written by the associate editor, a long-time colleague. It characterized him as "having the combined elements of a superior mentality and the spirit of humility that characterize all Christian gentlemen." It continued, "As a teacher, he was a genius. He could hold in a smooth persuasive manner the attention of his boys when imparting to them the fundamentals of an education, and by his exemplary life inspire the highest ideals of correct living."

Letters Addressed to Vernon
at
The North Carolina
State School for the Blind
Raleigh, North Carolina

1922—1924

Saturday A.M.
(Sept. 21, 1922)

MY DEAR VERNON,

I am wondering how you are, and how you got along on your way to Raleigh. Don't suppose you have formed an opinion as to how you like it yet, but I feel sure that, when you become acquainted, you will like it just fine. Have you seen Mrs. Bilyeu yet? Give her my very best regards.

Son, you must write to me real often and let me know all about everything, for you know I am deeply interested.

Harold and I are well, but we miss you badly. It's lonesome since you left, but guess Mama will soon be back. The Talberts[1] send love.

Am in a hurry this A.M. Write.

Your affectionate
DAD

Monday
(Sept. 23, 1922)

MY DEAR VERNON,

I was so glad to get your letter Saturday and to know that you were liking it so well. I also received a card from Mr. Lineberry[2] telling me of your safe arrival.

Harold and I are getting along fine, but we were very lonesome yesterday. We miss you so much. I look for Mama the last of this week. Guess you have heard from her.

The Talberts send love. Let me know if you need anything.

DAD

Thursday, Sept. 26, 1922

MY DEAR VERNON,

I was so glad to get your letter yesterday afternoon. I can hardly realize that it has been only one week today since you left here. Seems more like one month. You know it has been awfully

---

[1]Next-door neighbors.
[2]Superintendent of the North Carolina State School for the Blind.

lonesome at home by myself. I am on duty this week,[1] and when I get at home at night I find that Harold has already gone to bed at Mrs. T.V.'s [Talbert], so I haven't seen him since Monday morning, though I went by and said a few words to him last night as I went home. He is perfectly contented at T.V.'s.

Haven't begun work on my house yet. Expect Mr. Bob Hudson will remodel it for me. I expect to build the kitchen at the east end of the dining room, run a stairway to upper story, and finish two rooms up there for you boys. How will you like a room upstairs?

Vernon, I was sorry to hear that you had lost your money. I will send you some more and another knife. Either let Mrs. Bilyeu keep the money for you, or carry it with you all the time. Am anxious for you to improve your writing, spelling, and use of capitals.

Let me know who your teachers are, your friends, and all about your schoolwork and everything. And, Son, don't forget to pray and read your Bible every day.

Affectionately,
DAD

Friday A.M.
September 29 (1922)

MY DEAR SON,

I have just received a letter from your Aunt Bert saying that she had written to Mama to stay at Grandpa's until Tuesday, as she was counting on going there to see her the last of this week. I haven't heard from Mama since, so I don't know whether she will come home tonight as she had intended or not. But I will meet the train anyway if I don't hear from her today. You know I am getting so anxious to see them.

Hope you are still enjoying yourself at the school. You must work hard, be manly and kind, and try to make a splendid record

---

[1]"On duty" for a week, an officer at the Training School got the boys up at six AM, and was responsible for them until he put them to bed at eight PM. "Off duty" on alternate weeks, he had responsibilities with boys from breakfast through dinner.

there. I want to know all about your work in school and out and just everything.

　　With much love from

DAD

Wednesday A.M.
(Oct. 1, 1922)

MY DEAR VERNON,

　　How are you this nice, cool morning? I just imagine you are feeling fine. Such weather is just to my liking. Do hope it will be this nice next week when I go to see you. I can hardly wait for the time to come, for I want to see you dreadfully. It may be that I will get there in time to go with you to the Fair on Tuesday. If I don't I will see you Tuesday evening anyway.

　　I was mighty glad to get your letter last night. It was very interesting to me and your Mother. You know that we are always glad to hear from you and, Son, you must not neglect writing to us. I want you to write two or three times a week.

　　Vernon, you can sell your knife if you want to, and I will send or take you another. They are mighty good knives for the money.

　　I remember one Harris boy who was there while I was, but his name was Leon. Don't seem to remember any "Colonel" Harris. Is Mr. Cox there now? He once was bandmaster.

　　Elroy and Harold have been picking cotton for Mr. Garmon. Mr. Horton has got his new house about ready to live in. He expects to move this week. The Talberts are all well but Maude. She is having chills. You must be sure to write to Frank Pharr. And don't fail to spell it P-h-a-r-r.

　　Guess I will see you next week. Be good to the little blind boy of whom you were made guardian.

Affectionately,
DAD

We love you.

Thursday
(Oct., 1922)

DEAR VERNON,

Your very short note came day before yesterday. Of course I was glad to hear from you, but you never write any but very short letters. I think you might write me and your Mama a long letter sometimes. Have they removed tonsils yet? While I was away on vacation over one hundred of the boys here had theirs taken out. How are you getting along in school? I am anxious to have a good report from you. And are you liking cornet? I hope you are, and that you will work hard and some day you will be glad that you have done your best.

I was sorry to hear of the trouble Watts is having.

Do you need any money or anything? Let me know if you do. Can furnish all the knives you can sell. I love you.

DAD

October 30

MY DEAR VERNON,

We were mighty glad to get your letter last Friday. You know, son, we are so pleased that you are getting along so nicely, and that you like it there. We miss you a lot, but then time passes very rapidly and it won't be so very long till you can come home. I think you have fattened up considerably and when I see you again I expect to find a big change in you. I know it will benefit you a lot to have your tonsils removed.

They removed the tonsils from 100 boys here last week. They are all right now. Several boys have run away since I left, but they get them back without much trouble.

I went to Charlotte Sat. At Harrisburg[1] I saw William Sloop. He inquired about you. Said he had heard from you, and had answered your letter.

Elroy and Harold are in school and getting along nicely. R. H.[2]

---

[1]Community near Jackson Training School where Crook had been school principal and where Vernon had attended school.

[2]Roger.

is almost walking. We had his picture made and if they are good, will send one to you.

Am sending you another knife. If you can sell it for 75¢ or $1.00 will send you another—all you can sell. They are mighty good knives.

All join me in love to you. Write often.

Your loving father.

Tuesday, Nov. 14, '22

MY DEAR SON,

Your letter came yesterday and we were all so glad to hear from you. I think you are improving in your letter writing, as the form of your last letter and its composition were both good. I certainly am proud of the good grades you made in the tests on spelling and geography. Study hard, son, and learn all you can so that when you become a man you will be better prepared to earn a living and also to do more good here in the world. You are young yet, Vernon, and haven't learned, as I have, the great truth that one gets the best out of life and the most of its joys, only by close application to duty and by helpful service. I pray for you, my son, and trust that you will grow into a fine manhood.

I am so glad you like the cornet. If you can become a good bandsman it might be the means of your livelihood some day. Who knows but what you may have charge of the J.T.S. Band some time! I am most anxious for you to prepare yourself for usefulness.

We are getting along very well. Elroy's thumb has been quite sore, but the Dr. gave him some medicine that seems to be healing it up now. He and Harold appreciate the balloons you sent them. They said tell you "Thanks." Wish you could see Roger Hawley. He has grown quite a lot since you saw him. I don't see much of the Talbert's children these days as it is night when I get home and I've not been at home much on Sundays. Have been on duty every Sunday except last Sunday since I saw you. Last Sunday T.V., Shaw, and I went to Samarkand, the girls' school. Had a nice trip. Went by Star, but didn't stop.

We have about 280 boys at J.T.S. now. Haven't had but one

run away in some time. Mr. Hilton has left the school and his place in the bakery is being filed by a Mr. Spaugh from Valdese. Guinea Sheppard is back here. He ran away from Mr. White's and stole a car in Concord.

We have the outside of our house painted at last. It is white trimmed in brown and looks quite nice.

I will pay for gym shoes. Am sending you a check for $2.00. If you need more let me know. Give my love to Mrs. Bilyeu.

Affectionately,

DAD

P.S. I notice you spell *going* this way: *goeing.* Be sure to learn how to spell it right.

Friday A.M.
(Nov., 1922)

MY DEAR VERNON,

I was so glad to get a letter from Mrs. Bilyeu yesterday, and one from Mr. Lineberry too, saying that you were getting along splendidly after your operation. Am glad I didn't know about it until after it was over, as I would have been uneasy. I am sure it will do you lots of good.

We are all very well. Am in a hurry this A.M. Write just as soon as you can. I love you, old boy.

Affectionately,

DAD

Monday A.M.
Nov. 27, 1922

MY DEAR VERNON,

I am so anxious to hear from you. Certainly hope you are feeling all right and that the operation you have had will be a great benefit to you. I guess you are back in school by now. We are so glad your tonsils and adenoids are gone. Expect you will feel so much better and will fatten now.

Son, we appreciated your last letter very much. It was a nice long one, and those verses were good. Yes, indeed, we think of you every day, and pray that you may be kept well in body and heart. You must send us a copy of the verses you wrote and recited in school. I want to read them. I am very proud of you, boy.

We will be glad to have your friends come to see you any time they can. Be sure to have young Oats come.

Write as soon as you can.

With love,
DAD

(Nov. 28, 1922)

MY DEAR VERNON,

This is Tuesday evening and I felt sure I would hear from you today, but was disappointed. Son, I am very anxious to hear from you, and so is Mama. She was expecting a letter last night. Certainly hope you have recovered from operation, and that you will feel much better . . . .

I hope you will have a pleasant Thanksgiving. You know we have so much to be thankful for. Mama expects to send you a box of candy tomorrow.

Write to us often, Son.

With love,
DAD

Friday, Dec. 1, '22

MY DEAR VERNON,

I can't understand why we don't hear from you. The last letter we had from you was the one you wrote before your operation. Your mother and I are so anxious to hear from you.

We had a splendid thanksgiving at J.T.S. yesterday. Took the boys rabbit hunting in the A.M. They caught 24. At two o'clock we had barbecued pig. Played Rocky River Basketball team in the afternoon. Last night the Rotary Club of Mooresville came down and gave us a concert. It was fine.

Now Vernon, write to us *at once*.

With love,
DAD

December 2, 1922

My dear Son,

The last letter we had from you was written before your operation. We are very anxious to hear from you. Why don't you write, or get someone to write for you? Let us hear from you at once. And don't let it be so long anymore.

Hastily,
Dad

Monday, Dec. 4th, 1922

My dear Son,

We were mighty glad to get a letter from you Saturday and another yesterday. I guess the reason we have not been receiving your letters is because you did not put them in care of J.T.S.

Mighty glad you had such a nice time Thanksgiving Day. Believe I wrote you about the day here. Next will be Christmas. I am not expecting to find much difference when Christmas comes, as I will be on duty. Wish I could be with you. Mama and I will send you a box. How are your clothes holding out? Have you got a flashlight? If you haven't will send one.

Love from all,
Dad

P.S. In your last letter you spelled "goeing." It is "going."

(Monday, Dec. 16, 1922)

My dear Son,

Your letter was received yesterday (Sunday) and we were so glad to hear from our boy again, as it had been about two weeks since we had had a letter from you.

We are all well and looking forward to the coming of Christmas when, I hope, you and Mama may be together. She, Harold, and Roger expect to go to Grandpa's Saturday. Elroy and I will stay here. I have not heard from Mr. Lineberry yet, so I don't know whether he will let you go or not. Just as soon as you get this letter, see him and find out if you can go, if only for one day. Grandpa is very feeble, and I would like for you to see him, besides, it will cost less for you to go to Sanford than for the family to go to Raleigh. Let me know what he says.

I am sending you $5.00 for your Christmas present from the family. *Be sure* to save enough out of it to go to Sanford if you get to go. If you don't go, I want you to use some of it to get yourself a Bible. Be sure to get one with large print.

I have also taken out for you a share of Building and Loan stock. It costs 25¢ a week to pay for it, but at the end of 331 weeks it will be worth $100. I have paid up until Jan. 1st. I bought a share for Elroy and Harold also.

I hope you will have a pleasant Christmas. Let me know *at once* what Mr. Lineberry says.

Lots of love,

DAD

P.S. Let me know what your shoes cost.

(Dec., 1922)

MY DEAR SON,

I am wishing you much happiness during the glad Christmas-time, and through all the new year. Am sending you a sweater under separate cover, and am enclosing ck. for $1.00 herewith.

Am very busy, but will write a *letter* soon. We appreciate the nice long letters we get from you.

I love you, boy.

Hastily,

DAD

P.S. Mabel is going to send you something, so I think you ought to send her a little present. Please do.

Dec. 30, 1922

MY DEAR VERNON,

This, I suppose, will be the last letter I write to you during the year 1922. And as the year lies "a-dying," I think of some of the joys it has given us. On the whole it has been a very good year, and the Lord has blessed us in taking care of us through all of the 365 days. As the New Year comes in, with its opportunities and obligations, I hope that it will bring us happiness. I hope that we may set for ourselves *high ambitions* and that we may live and act worthily.

Well, I must tell you something of our Christmas. From the enclosed menu, you may see what we had for dinner that day. Saturday night we had our Xmas tree. It was beautiful and our Christmas entertainment was fine. We all got well-filled "pokes." All the home folks but Roger and Mrs. T.V. were here. Our kids and the Talberts had a tree at home Friday night. Each one got something. Santa was good to me. He gave me several presents. Mama gave me a pair of gloves and some handkerchiefs; Elroy gave me sleeve holders; Harold, some cigars; Mabel, some smoking tobacco; Mr. Fisher, a nice tie; Mr. Roger, a box of handkerchiefs; Howard (one of the boys), a nice tie; Barns (an older boy), a knife. I gave Mama a fountain pen, Elroy a flashlight, Harold a windmill, and Roger a fuzzy dog.

We have not started back to school yet. Guess we will go Tuesday. We are killing hogs at the school today. Wish you could have some of the sausages.

Son, I am anxious to know if you got the check and sweater I sent you, and the package of cake and candy from home. The only letter we have had from you in over two weeks was written Dec. 24. Don't neglect writing to us.

This is poor scribbling, but am writing on my knees and its a poor job.

With best wishes for a happy New Year, and love from all,

DAD

How are you getting along with cornet?

(Jan., 1923)

MY DEAR SON,

Your card, the first I had heard from you since Mama left, was received tonight (Friday), and I was so very glad to hear from my boy again.

I am glad you had such a nice time Christmas. What all did you get? We, Elroy and I, had a very nice time. He got a knife, dominoes, and lots of eats. Mama gave me some bedroom slippers, Elroy gave me a tie and Harold a pair of cuff links. A boy at the school also gave me cuff links. But it has been a long, lonely time with Mama and the boys away. I haven't slept at home since they left. I guess they will go to see you Monday. How I wish I could go too! But it is impossible.

The light is poor, so I can't see to write very well. I hope to get a long letter from you soon, and have a good report of you from Mama. Son, it makes me glad to know that you are taking an active part in prayer meetings. Keep it up.

What was the name of your play? Did you have a part in it?

Hope to have a *long* letter next time. May you have a happy and prosperous new year.

Lots of love,
DAD

January 10, 1923

MY DEAR VERNON,

We were very glad to get your letter last night, and to know that you are getting along so well. We always look forward to receiving your letters. They give us much pleasure, Son, and we are proud of you and the improvement you are making. I am glad that you love poetry, and I hope that you may some day become a writer of beautiful poetry yourself. But, Vernon, don't neglect your lessons. Remember that they *come first*. Your spelling and English both need to be improved. And I am very anxious for you to succeed with cornet. Work hard with it and master it. It might be the means of your livelihood some day . . . .

Give my love to Mrs. Bilyeu. Will write again soon. Am sending ck. for $1.00. Spend it wisely.

DAD

January 16, 1923

MY DEAR SON,

Your letter was received Friday, and, as usual, we were all glad to hear from you. Your letters mean a great deal to your mother and me. We look forward to them with great pleasure. You know, almost the first thing they say to me at night when I get home is: "Did you hear from Vernon today?" You are improving in letter writing and in spelling, and also in typewriting, I think. How many words can you write a minute? Do you use the touch system?

Am very sorry that you had to give up cornet. It was a hope of mine that you could succeed at it. Do you think you tried as hard as you could?

Would you like to try violin or guitar? Nothing would please me more than for you to learn some musical instrument, and I think you might learn guitar. If you can learn to play it, I will get you a nice one.

Do you sing? You should. I hope you will learn to sing well. Then you will find that it will afford you much pleasure and bring popularity.

Do you have occasion to use your point slate any? And can you read point any more rapidly than you could when you left? What books do you study? Are you getting along well in arithmetic? You know I am very anxious for you to succeed.

We are all well. Lots of love.

DAD

P.S. Let me know if you need anything.

Jan. 31st 1923

MY DEAR VERNON,

This is the last half of the last day of January, and I will use a part of it to answer your letter which I received this A.M. I certainly was glad to hear from you again. Your letters are always a great pleasure to us, Son. I want you to be a little more careful with your typewriting. You hit the wrong key 23 times. You know how that makes a word look—for instance "gas" for *has*, "knoe" for *know*. You misspelled *Daddy, examination, two-fifths, Miss Fisher, slept, Pen,* a step or *two, wouldn't, accomplished,* State School for the *Blind.* That is 10 words. You spelled them this way: Dady—examanitions—penn—a step or too—too fifth—Mrs. Fisher—slep—woulden't—accomploshed—School for the blind. You failed to use capital letters eleven times, and lots of punctuation marks. Try to improve your next, won't you?

Last night was so rainy and, as I have a very bad cold, I did not go home. Just before I went to bed Mr. Grier returned from Chapel Hill. He brought Bones back with him. I guess you remember Bones? He certainly has grown a lot, and is a very fine dog. He belongs to the school now.

Vernon, I have the nicest pup—a fox terrier—that you ever saw. She is a beauty. She is white and brown. What would you suggest for a name for her?

Roger is some better of whooping cough. The rest of us are all well exept for my bad cold. Sore eyes are better. The neighbors are all, generally, well.

I know that you enjoy the nice walks, and the interesting things you see. Your experience reminds me of some of mine when I was there. I certainly wish I could be with you on some of your rambles.

I am rather disappointed at the low mark you made on exams, but I feel sure your next will be higher. But I am vastly proud of the success you are making with piano. Stick to it and master it, Son, and it will be a help and a pleasure to us all. And I am also pleased to have you interested in debating, and YMCA work. That's it. It makes me proud of you. Always do your part well, but don't neglect your schoolwork for anything. Write soon.

DAD

(Wed., Feb., 1923)

MY DEAR VERNON,

We were very glad indeed to get your letter yesterday (Tuesday). We are so pleased to know that you are getting along so well with all your work. You must always do your best for if you get along well I will try to send you to college. I hope that by the time you are 18 you will be through at Raleigh.

We are all well and getting along just fine. The boys will be out of school this week. They are very glad of that.

Excuse this note. I'm very busy today.

Lots of love,
DAD

DEAR SON,

We were delighted to get your letter and report day before yesterday. Your letter was very nicely written. Am glad to see the improvement. And your report was pretty good. You know that your mother and I always look for a lot of A's on your report. Try to keep neat so that you may get A on neatness next time. Look after your hair, teeth, and nails and keep shoes shined and clothes brushed. I was so proud to see A on deportment.

Roger is rather troublesome with whooping cough. The rest of children are well.

Will write more in a few days.

Hastily,
DAD

Feb. 14, '23

MY DEAR SON,

I have been thinking all this week that I would write to you and have in fact begun one or two letters, but have been so busy that I just could not get caught up with all I had to do. We were very glad indeed to get your nice letter Tuesday. We all appreciate the verses you wrote. They show that you love us, and that is what we want above almost anything. The verses were good. When you come home I will teach you what I know about poetic form. I haven't had time to write many verses lately. Here is a jingle I just jotted down. But let me explain before I write the verse. Mrs. Duckett has fallen out with Miss Goodman over the cream. She accuses Miss Goodman of drinking all the cream. Here goes:

> Once there was a woman named Duckett
> With a stomach as big as a bucket;
> On cream she did feast
> Till a mean little beast
> Came up to the table and "tuck" it.

I have just compiled a record book for the schoolroom, and am having it published. It will be a great help in keeping the reports.

Mama reads every night, just as she did when you were here. Some of the books we have recently read are: *Under Fire* by Parker; *Clan Call* by Liebe; *The House of Mohun* by Gibbs. We are reading *Corporal Cameron* by Ralph Connor now. It's fine.

Son, if you need anything, let me know. Don't wear the shoes if your toes stick out. Wear your others, and I will send you some money to get more. Just let me know when you need them.

Am glad you are upstairs now. Be a good boy, and don't forget to read the Bible and pray every day.

Am sending you $1.00. Let me know if you need shoes or cap.

Lots of love,
DAD

(Feb., 1923)

MY DEAR VERNON,

I haven't got much time to write this A.M. but will scribble you a few lines anyway as Mama is washing and won't have time.

We haven't had any school since Friday of last week on account of the flu. There have been over a hundred cases of it at J.T.S. Mr. Talbert, Lee White, Hobby, Kinnett, and Horton have had it. Three of the boys had pneumonia, and one of them died last week. He was taken with flu first. His name was Corbett and he lived at Elizabeth City.

Yes, I knew Sam Davis. He certainly can rattle a piano.

Just as soon as I can, will write a long letter. We are very well.

Lots of love,
DAD

Saturday (Feb., 1923)

MY DEAR SON,

Just a line to let you know that we are so anxious to hear from you. Can't you get one of your friends to write us at least a card to tell us how you are? The last we heard from you was a card from Mrs. B. over a week ago. I do hope that you are about well of the measles by now, and that you can soon resume your regular work.

We are all well. Roger is cutting teeth and is a little fretful. Elroy and Harold are getting along fairly well in school this year. Mabel has not gone to school any in over a week because of a very bad cold. She is some better I think, tho' I haven't seen her this week as I'm on duty and you know what time I get home.

Did I tell you that we have a new bandmaster at J.T.S.? He is a Mr. Stebbins, from the New York Training School. Can't expect to like him as well as I did Mr. Lawrence.

Did you get the shoes I sent you? And the box Mama sent? Hope the shoes fit O.K. and that you like them. Be careful with them so you will have a nice pair at commencement.

Lots of love from
DAD

Do you need any money?

Feb. 27, '23

MY DEAR BOY,

Your letter which came last night was the first I had had from you in over a week. We were getting uneasy about you. Don't neglect writing to us.

Am delighted that you are getting along so well. Your grade on the tests was just fine. When you get good marks you make us very happy. Are you able to play anything on the piano yet?

I had a letter from Uncle Alex last week. He has moved to southern Mississippi. He has bought a farm out there. Guess it will be a long time before I see him again.

Are both pairs of your shoes worn out? Let me know. Wear your best pair. Will send money next week to get you another pair, or get them myself. What no. [number] do you wear?

Hastily,
DAD

(March, 1923)

MY DEAR SON,

Your letter and report came yesterday, and as usual we were glad to hear from you again. We also had a card yesterday from your Aunt Vannie. She said she sees you on Sundays right often.

Fred Pigford, whom you saw not long ago, is a distant cousin of ours. I should like very much to see him and Bernard Williamson.

I am glad that you are taking part in a debating society. It will be of much help to you. Do you have prayer meetings at the school? And do you attend church and Sunday School at 1st Baptist Church now? Are you enjoying the reading this year?

Son, your report was not altogether as good as I hoped to find it. "D" on typewriting is very low. "C" on grammar, history, geography, and piano is not a very high mark. You will gladden my heart, partner, if the next report shows an improvement. Well, since I have started, I might as well tell you that I don't approve of you buying secondhand clothes from the boys, especially where you have to go in debt for them. Let me know any time you need anything and, if possible, you shall have it. It is nice for you to buy and sell candy. Keep your slippers until you come home.

Am writing to Mr. Lineberry today. Hope to hear from him real soon. Will let you know what he says. I wish I could go to Grandpa's too, but can't.

With lots of love,
DAD

(1) Never buy anything you don't need simply because it is cheap. Whenever you need clothing or anything let me know.

(2) Don't go in debt. Whenever you contract debts you promise what you haven't got and may never have. I will gladly try to supply you with a reasonable amount of spending money.

(3) Don't spend your money foolishly. Learn to save, it will be worth a great deal to you to learn this lesson well.

(4) Learn to economize. Only the rich can have whatever they want, and there are many things money can't buy.

(March, 1923)

MY DEAR VERNON,

A letter just received from Mrs. Bilyeu informs me that you have measles. Now, son, do just as she tells you, and be especially careful of your eyes. *Don't read at all.* If you take good care of yourself you will soon be all right. But do be careful and don't take cold. I know Mrs. Bilyeu will be good to you.

We are all well except for colds. I have it very bad.

With lots of love,
DAD

March 14, '23

MY DEAR VERNON,

Am sending you a nice pair of slippers by today's mail. Hope you will receive them and that they will fit you all right. Be careful with them and if they don't fit return them at once and I will exchange them. They are nice ones, and you must keep them clean and shining, and don't wear them every day. And, Son, look after your teeth and nails, keep your neck and ears clean, keep your hair cut when it needs it and combed and brushed nicely all the time. Try to get *A* on neatness.

I hope you have recovered from measles before now. We are all so anxious to hear from you, and as soon as you get able, write to us. It seems like a long time since we heard from you.

We are all very well now. Roger has at last got about over the whooping cough. Mrs. Talbert has been very sick for a week or two but is some better now, but not able to sit up yet. Mabel, too, has been sick for a few days, but is all right now.

I had a letter from your Uncle Alex last week. They seem to like their new home in Mississippi just fine. We have not heard from Aunt Mary in some time, but she was well when she wrote last.

Mama sent you a box yesterday. Hope you got it. Did you read the verses we sent some days ago?[1] They were published in the *Observer* and also in the Sanford paper.

Write to us just as soon as you can.

Lots of love,
DAD

---

[1]This poem was published in the Charlotte *Observer* on February 23, 1923.

28

O Son of Mine

I wish for thee, O son of mine,
When thou art grown to man's estate,
And passed beyond that golden gate
Which shuts upon thy youth's confine,
That thou mayest hold inviolate
Thy simple faith in things divine.

I wish for thee, O son of mine,
When into manhood thou art grown,
That Truth and Right thou mayest enthrone
Within thy heart's most hallowed shrine;
That thou mayest keep thy life a-tone
With Love and Charity benign.

I wish for thee, O son of mine,
The happiness that wisdom brings—
The length of days, the peace which springs
From knowledge of the good, the fine.
I wish for thee the heart that clings
In child-like trust to God's design.

(March 19, 1923)

My dear Vernon,

We were so very glad to get your letter Sunday A.M., and also the Braille letter Saturday, but haven't got it all figured out yet. Please don't write any more point, unless you write another way. I know you were glad to get out of the sickroom. Hope you will not have any more sickness this year.

Your birthday is Sunday, and Mama and I are sending a little check for a present. You can buy whatever you want as a present from us.

Will write more soon.

Dad

MY DEAR SON,

This is the last day of the month, and is as cold as it has been any time this winter. It doesn't seem at all like spring, yet the fruit trees are gorgeous in their bright blossoms. I certainly would be glad to see it turn warmer. I fear the fruit has already been killed in this section.

Tomorrow is Easter Sunday, and I hope you will have a joyous time. Guess you will go to church and Sunday School, and I imagine there will be some special music for the occasion. Will you have a big dinner, lots of eggs, etc.? Elroy and Harold attended an egg hunt at White Hall yesterday. Elroy found seven and Harold three I think. Eastertime is always a pleasant time at J.T.S. The boys get lots of eggs and have a good time. Easter, being the Resurrection Day—the day when our Lord rose from the grave—should be a joyous occasion to us.

Nearly all the flu patients have got well here. There are only 15 or 20 still in bed. We had two nurses and several doctors to attend the sick, but in spite of the very best care, one boy answered the Great Summons and passed away. He was a boy whom all here liked.

Mama and Roger are not very well. He—Roger—is cutting teeth and Mama has cold, but they both are up. They seemed better this morning. The rest of us are very well. Mabel has not been able to return to school yet, but is not confined to her bed.

Vernon, who is your Sunday School teacher? And who is the superintendent? Do you ever go to church Sunday nights? Who is pastor of the First Baptist Church? I hope you attend regularly, and that you read and study the Word of God. Don't forget to pray.

One of our boys, Funderburk, from Monroe, got his leg broken yesterday while playing ball. Was taken to the hospital in Concord last night. Vass Fields (you know him) got his collarbone broken a few days ago. He is getting along fine now.

Well, I must have lessons, so goodbye.

DAD

MY DEAR VERNON,

We didn't get the mail yesterday (Sunday), and I feel like there is one in the office from you, but I will write you a few lines this morning and not wait to see if I get one from you. We are all well and getting along fine. Roger is a fine boy and is as full of life as can be. I do wish you could see him. Elroy and Harold have grown a lot since you left, and Elroy, especially, is stout. They are getting along fine in school. Their school will be out in two more weeks.

A baby was born at Mrs. Talbert's Friday night. It lived only a day. Was buried at the Ridge. Mabel has not been able to go back to school. She is not at all strong. She came out to see us yesterday as usual. Dixon spent the night with Elroy one night last week.

Do you go to church and Sunday School every Sunday? Who is your Sunday School teacher?

Are you still taking piano? I didn't see any mark for piano on your report. But I did see the disorder mark. I certainly hope you will never get another. Otherwise, your report was pretty good.

I am so anxious to see you, Son. Seems like we can't wait till school is out. But it won't be long now.

Be good. Lots of love.

DAD

Wednesday
(After Easter, 1923)

MY DEAR VERNON,

Mama received your letter yesterday and we were all so glad to hear from you. That was a splendid letter, and the Easter verse at the beginning was very good.

Glad to know that you had a pleasant time Easter. We, too, enjoyed it. Last night we had an entertainment at the school. George Lawrence and his brother, Rev. Alfred Lawrence, and two of the Chapel Hill professors were here.

This note is just to let you know that we received your letter and to ask you to always be punctual hereafter in writing to us.

Affectionately,

DAD

Wednesday, April 25, 1923

MY DEAR SON,

Your mother and I both received letters from you yesterday, and you don't know how glad we were to hear from you. It had been just two weeks since we had had a letter from you. Guess some of your letters got misplaced.

We are all well and happy. Roger H. is a sight. He goes over to Mr. Horton's right often by himself. Is talking just a little. Elroy and Harold are in the play to be given at White Hall at close of school. Frances is in it, too.

It is not long now until May 31st and I can hardly wait. We want to see you so bad. Vernon, be *sure* to bring all your clothes, shoes, etc. Your old shoes will be of use this summer.

I am glad for you to go with Mr. Cox and it is fine for him to like you so well. Don't neglect your schoolwork for anything. I expect to send you to college when you get through there and I want you to be well prepared by the time you are eighteen. I expect to teach you Latin this summer.

I am sending you a check for $1.00. Don't spend it foolishly. You know money is hard to get and harder to keep.

Be careful about your spelling and capital letters. When you put School for the Blind on envelope, *Blind* should begin with *B.* The way to spell Mabel is not "Mable." The names of the days of the week, Monday, Tuesday, etc., begin with capitals.

Lots of love,

DAD

May 15, 1923

MY DEAR SON,

Your letter written Sunday to your mother has just been received. It was a good letter, Boy, and much appreciated. I was indeed sorry to hear of the sad death of Mrs. Simpson. I remember her very pleasantly. Will Mr. Simpson stay on at his home or move in with one of his boys?

Yes, I shall be glad for you to see something of your friend in Concord this summer. Invite him to come to see you.

We are all well, and counting the days till you come home. We want to see you. Guess you have grown a lot since you left.

Son, it seems to me that you spend money pretty fast. It hasn't been long since I sent you a dollar. Am sorry you didn't have any to pay on flowers. Am sending you another dollar. Take care of it and don't spend it foolishly. This is all I have time to write today.

> With love,
> DAD

> Saturday
> (May, 1923)

DEAR SON,

I have just received your letter and though I'm anxious to see you at the earliest moment, I don't think it would be best for you to travel by yourself as you would have to change cars in Greensboro. So just wait till the others come. But I can hardly wait for the time to pass.

> Lots of love,
> DAD

Will meet you Friday.

> Saturday
> (Fall, 1923, following return
> from summer vacation)

MY DEAR VERNON,

As I have a few minutes before lessons are ready this morning, and as I know you want to hear from us, I will write you a few lines. I hope you got to Raleigh safe and that you like your new place. And, too, I hope your feet did not bother you so much. Who met you at Concord? Who are your roommates? Are most of your classmates back? You must tell me just everything when you write.

All are well at home, but we miss you so much. You know, Son, I am expecting great things from you. My hopes are in my boys.

Mr. Johnson has not returned to the school yet. We look for him any day now. You heard before you left, I think, that the operation was successful. I shall be glad for Johnson to get back, as I can't get my vacation until he returns.

Lots of love from all. Mama will write when we hear from you.

DAD

October 5, '23

MY DEAR SON,

Your letter and card have been received, and needless to say, we were so glad to hear from you. Yes, you have been moving around quite a bit since you got there. Have you got settled permanently yet? Glad you like your new quarters.

What are your studies this year? Are Mrs. Bilyeu, Mr. Cox, and Miss Gertie there this year? Remember me to them when you see them, and to Mr. and Mrs. Reaves and Mr. Blair, also.

Mr. Johnson got back Tuesday. His baby is getting along fine. Mr. Cloer left the school Monday. I haven't got my vacation yet. Don't look like I can get off. I did not get to go to T.V.'s birthday dinner. I went to the Exposition at Charlotte Wed. night. It was very good. Mr. Groover took T.V., Lee White, and me. Enjoyed it very much.

Today is Roger's birthday, and tomorrow is mine. I will be 38. I wanted to be at home for dinner and eat some chicken but guess I'll be here and eat Irish potatoes instead.

It is time to have lessons.

Lots of love,
DAD

(October, 1923)

DEAR VERNON,

Your cards to Mama and me were received last week. Sorry that you have such a bad cold. I, too, have a bad one. The rest are well.

I know you are busy since you began to work in the shop. But you must find time occasionally to write us a letter. We have had two letters from you since you left, and several cards.

Mr. Wilson moved into his house Sat. Mr. Russell has begun building on his lot, and Mr. Jones Pharr expected to build before spring.

Son, be a good boy, guard against your temper, and don't use bad language.

Affectionately,
DAD

Monday (Oct., 1923)

MY DEAR SON,

We received a letter from you Saturday. Very glad to hear from you. We are all well.

The whole school will go to the Fair at Concord tomorrow. Will walk over.

Wish I could go to see you this week, but can't get off.

I enclose check for $2.00. *Buy a pair of overalls for shop.*

Hastily,
YOUR FATHER

Saturday A.M. (Nov., 1923)

MY DEAR SON,

We were glad to get your letter yesterday. You never said anything about the check I sent you. Did you get it? Be very careful about how you spend money. Buy whatever you need and don't waste it.

We are all well. We added only one room, the kitchen, to our house. Vernon, please don't spell "going" this way: "goeing." There is no "e" in it.

Write often.
DAD

(Soon after Nov. 11, 1923)

MY DEAR VERNON,

After a two weeks vacation I am back at work again. I certainly enjoyed being at home. I went to Charlotte to the Armistice Day celebration, and took Harold to see Dr. Brawley last Sat. and again yesterday. Am so glad to say that his vision can be improved by glasses. Hope they will come the last of the week.

I cut a lot of wood and cleaned off the new ground while at home. My hands are all blistered, but I certainly enjoyed the work.

Son, I hope you are well and studying hard. You will soon be a man, and we want you to be a good, useful one, and a follower of the Master. Read the Bible and don't forget to pray. You don't know how much I love you.

DAD

(Wed., Nov. 28, 1923)

MY DEAR BOY,

Your letter to Mama came yesterday, and we were all so glad to hear from you. I haven't time this a.m. to write much, but I just must wish for you a pleasant time tomorrow—Thanksgiving Day. One of the things for which I am very thankful this Thanksgiving season is that God has blessed me with four fine boys. I feel constrained to sing with the psalmist, "Bless the Lord, O my soul: and all that is within me, bless his holy name."

I intended to send you a nice box of candy today, but could not get off to go to town, so am sending $1.00 instead.

I love you, Son. Write to me soon and tell me all about your Thanksgiving.

DAD

(Before Christmas, 1923)

MY DEAR SON,

Mama and I were delighted to receive your good letter yesterday. You have made wonderful improvement in letter writing. We are proud of you, Boy. And it was good news you gave us, Son, about the meetings you smaller boys are conducting. We are glad that you are interested in things that are really worth-while, and especially in service for the Master. I know it will do you and the others much good.

I shall be very glad for you to join the society. Please do. And always do your part just as well as you can.

Have your chain fixed. It won't cost much.

We are practicing this a.m. for our Christmas exercises, and I'm so busy that I can't write any more this time.

Lots of love,
DAD

goeing—going.

Jan. Thursday (1924)

MY DEAR VERNON,

Though it is almost school time, I will write just a few lines any-way. You know I never write at night.

Your letter to Mama was received day before yesterday, and I think she is going to answer tomorrow. Roger has a very bad cold—almost had the croup last night. He had high fever and was delirious all night. Think he is some better this morning.

I wrote Mr. Lineberry that I consented to the proposed opera-tion on your eye, and I certainly hope it will do you good. Is it your best eye? If the operation is successful and relieves you of double vision, I may have a similar operation on mine as I am bothered with the same trouble. I shall be very anxious about you, Son, and want you to send me word every day how you are.

I went to Charlotte last week one night to hear Rev. Billy Sunday, who is holding a meeting there. Mr. Groover took W. W. and me. Wish you could hear him. He is a great preacher.

Hope you can hear Mr. Ham[1] often. He, too, is a wonderful preacher. Do you attend Jack Ellis's church?[2] I hope you will get to talk with him and tell him who you are. He was once a near neighbor of mine, and a good friend.

---

[1]M. F. Hamm, evangelist.
[2]Pullen Memorial Baptist Church, Raleigh, North Carolina.

Did you prove that ships are more useful to mankind than trains? I should like to hear you boys debate.

With lots of love, I am,

DAD

Jan. 28, 1924

MY DEAR SON,

I am so glad that the operation on your eye has been performed, and I certainly hope that it will benefit you. Am anxious to know how you are getting along, and if your eyesight is any better. How long did you have to stay in a darkened room? Did he, the Dr., remove the lens? You know we want to hear all about it.

Yesterday was such a glorious day. I came up to the school for Sunday School, but spent the rest of the day at home or walking. Mama and Harold went to West Concord for preaching. After dinner I took a nap, then Mama, Harold, Roger, and I went to walk. We went to the Overhead Bridge. My Sundays at home are very happily spent.

I certainly would like to hear you play the piano. Am sorry that you did not get to play in the recital, and also that you did not get to take your exams; but don't worry, for I know you will do your best anyway.

Lots of love,
DAD

(Feb., 1924)

DEAR VERNON,

Under separate cover is some printed information which will about cover the ground of inquiry.

There was no administration building until after Mr. Boger[1] came. To him belongs the credit of expanding the school capacity of from 60 to 520. Adm. [Administration] building burned Sept. 8, 1922. Tablet on new bldg. is as follows:

---

[1]Superintendent of Jackson Training School.

Erected in memory
of
James William Cannon
By His Wife
To Aid the Jackson Training School in Its Big Purpose
and Service in the Giving of a Chance to the Boys of
the State Who Need Its Care and Protection.
1922

First boy admitted was Worth Hatch of Burlington.

DAD

Feb. 11, '24

MY DEAR VERNON,

Your letter was received yesterday and, as usual, I was glad to hear from you. Am so much in hopes that the operation will benefit your eyes. Let me know every few days how they are, and take good care of yourself.

We are all well except Roger has a very bad cold. Mama and I went to Charlotte yesterday with Willie White to hear Billy Sunday, but we couldn't get in the Tabernacle at all. There were 5,000 people turned away, they say. But we enjoyed the trip just the same. Last night was the last of his meeting at Charlotte. He is a wonderful man and I believe that he did a lot of good. There were a great many professions.

Wish I could have heard the debate on the Bonus bill. Personally, I am opposed to it except for disabled soldiers.

Your last report, except for so many disorder marks, was better than the first. I sincerely hope that those will be the last that you ever get. And I shall look for your next to be even better than this.

We are not having very many runaways now. One boy got as far toward Florida as Charlotte last week.

Lots of love,
DAD

March 4th, 1924

MY DEAR VERNON,

We were all glad to get your letter Friday, and to know that you are getting along so well. You write very interesting letters, Son, and we are proud of you. Seems like I can't wait until school is out to see you. I love you and think of you every day. I hope the time will pass rapidly until you come home. How much do you weigh? How are your clothes holding out? If you need anything let me know. Keep your hair cut as often as is needed, keep it combed, and keep your teeth clean, and your shoes shined.

I would like to hear you boys debate. I believe that if Congress could, and would, pass a compulsory school attendance law illiteracy would soon vanish from the U.S. Let me know whether you won or not, and if you have time, send me an outline of your speech, mentioning the points you made.

I know you enjoyed going to the Hamm meeting. Has it closed yet? We heard a wonderful sermon over the radio last night, and also yesterday morning. Dr. Little, of the First Baptist Church of Charlotte, was broadcasted yesterday A.M., and last night we heard a man from Kansas City. We made up the money to buy a splendid radio for 2nd cottage.

Mama and the boys are very well. They and Mabel and Maude came up last night to hear the sermon.

It is time to have lessons, so goodbye.

DAD

Aunt Mary has been very sick. Heart trouble. Write to her.

March 14, '24

MY DEAR SON,

Am sending stamps and a little spending money. Glad to get your letter yesterday. I hope you can soon go without the dark glasses. We are all well, except that I have a very bad cold.

Are you writing any verses this year? I have not written any at all. I have been spending all my spare time in writing a translation of Sallust—just to keep my Latin fresh—because I had never read Sallust. If you write any more send me a copy please.

We have at last got our radio paid for and enjoy it very much. We have it in the boys' sitting room at 2nd.

Had a letter from your Uncle Alex yesterday. They are getting along fine. His address is Richton, Miss. R.F.D. Write to him or Thelma some time. School time.

DAD

March 28 (1924)

MY DEAR VERNON,

It has been nearly two weeks since we heard from you and we are getting uneasy. Certainly hope you are well, and that your eyes are better. Do you still wear the dark glasses?

Your Mama sent you a beautiful birthday cake Monday, and I sent you a copy of *The Path to Home.* Some of the poems in it are so pretty that I wanted you to read them.

Roger Hawley has been right sick for two days. If he is no better by evening I will call the Dr. He seemed a little better this A.M. There are about 30 cases of measles at the school. They have turned 4th cottage into a hospital for them.

Hope to hear from you today. Let me know if you need anything, stockings, cap, or anything.

Lots of love,
DAD

P.S. Please give Mr. Lineberry the enclosed check for shoe repair.

April 2, 1924

MY DEAR VERNON,

On the same day that we received your last letter I wrote to you, so I guess you wonder whether we received your letter or not. As usual, we were very glad to hear from you, and especially glad to know that you made such excellent marks on exams. How are your eyes? Do you still have to wear dark glasses?

Mama intended to write to you today but asked me to write instead, as Roger is so much trouble. He has been right sick for over a week with lagrippe, but is better now. We had Drs. Patterson and King with him. He is much better now.

We have about 70 cases of measles at J.T.S. All doing well.

And Jno. [John] Russell has a baby girl. They are very happy. Glad you like the poems, and enjoyed the cake.

With much love,
DAD

(April 2, 1924)

MY DEAR SON,

Although I wrote to you this morning, I am writing again in reply to your letter of the 31st, which I have just received.

To speak frankly, I am not in sympathy with your tale of woe. You are entirely wrong. The school officials have a perfect right (since they stand *in loco parentis* to the children there) to open and read all mail. They have good reason to do this, you may be sure, and if yours is opened and read, I am convinced that they have a good reason for so doing. If you continue the movement, you will bring disaster upon yourself. What if you are not allowed to roam the streets as formerly, you must obey rules! They have perfect moral and legal right to make such rules.

If you value my advice, you will *obey rules;* you will do the right in so far as you know it; you will always conduct yourself with proper respect to those who are in authority over you; you will at all times be a gentleman.

Now Son, with a heart full of love for you, I beg that you drop the revolt. It will get you nowhere, but into disgrace. If you ask Mr. Lineberry in a gentlemanly way why your letters are opened, you might be enlightened. It would cause me great sorrow to have you expelled for being insubordinate. Remember, "The way of the transgressor is hard." Please don't "slip" any more letters, and if you are carrying on a correspondence with someone contrary to rules, please drop it. Need I say more? If this saves you from trouble, I shall be thankful.

Sorrowfully,
YOUR FATHER

April 10, '24

MY DEAR SON,

I am enclosing check for $1.00. Thought maybe you would be needing stockings or handkerchiefs or something.

We are all tolerably well now. Roger and I have both been sick with grippe or flu, but are much better. I never stopped work, but R. H. was laid up for a week. The rest are well.

A Mr. Alexander is running a store at Mr. Talbert's place. He seems to be a very nice man. Elroy and Harold are going with him over to the Morehead place this P.M.

Hope you are well. I had a letter from Mr. Lineberry last week. He said that very likely another operation would be necessary on your eye.

Son, I love you, and I expect great things from you. One of the things I expect is that you will make the very most of your opportunity to get an education.

DAD

Wednesday A.M.
(April, 1924)

DEAR VERNON,

Mama intended to write to you this A.M. but I forgot to take her any envelopes last night, so for fear she doesn't get to write, I will. I am glad to say that we are all much better of colds than when I last wrote. Roger is all right again. And all the boys who had measles at J.T.S. are getting along nicely. Among those of No. 2 who had measles was O'Quinn.[1] I guess you remember him. Aunt Mary has been very sick for some time. Has been confined to her bed for more than a month. That is why she has not written to you. I am anxious to go to see her.

Those girls certainly had a narrow escape from drowning. Son, I want you to learn to swim, but do be careful and always keep your nerve. Every one should learn to swim, I think. Tho I can't do much at it myself.

Did I tell you that a Mr. Alexander was running a store at Mr. Talbert's stand? He seems to be a pretty nice man—is a disabled soldier. Another Mr. Alexander is living in Mr. Pharr's house. He (Mr. Pharr) returned yesterday from Moore Co. where he has been for several months.

---

[1]The cottages, housing 30 boys each, were identified by numbers. Crook was stationed at No. 2.

The Talberts gave a weinie roast for Frances and the girls of her class last Sat. evening. The girls came in wagons, and two of them were standing up in the wagon and fell out. One was hurt pretty badly, but not seriously.

What grade will you be in next year? I wish you could make a grade at home this summer. Ask Mr. Griffin what you would have to study to do that. And ask him if you stand a satisfactory exam on those subjects at the beginning of next term if you can pass up one grade. Will be so glad to see you. Write.

Affectionately,
DAD

(May, 1924)

MY DEAR VERNON,

It is less than a month now before you come home, and as the time draws nearer the days seem longer and longer. I certainly do want to see you. I had a letter from Mr. Lineberry last week stating that school will close the 6th, and that you would be home about the 7th.

Yes, I want you to go to the picnic. I will send you some money in a few days. I am very proud of the excellent grades you made last month. It makes us very happy to get good reports from you.

Have you found out whether they will permit you to pass up a grade if you make it at home this summer? If they will let you I will get the textbooks you need.

I love you, my boy, and want to see you very badly.

Affectionately,
YOUR OLD DAD

(Spring, 1928)

MY DEAR VERNON,

Am enclosing ck. for $25, a loan from your B.&L., to buy you a suit, and engage room at University.[2] Are you sure you can get

---

[1]The letters from the fall of 1924, when Vernon returned to the School for the Blind, until the spring of 1929, just prior to his graduation from the School, have been lost. Three letters from the spring of 1928 have been preserved, and appear below.

[2]The University of North Carolina at Chapel Hill.

the $200.00 from the school? I do hope you can.

I have in my bid with Mr. Boger to get off to go to see you graduate and I think I can go, though not sure yet.

We have been attending the Gypsy Smith[3] meeting in Concord and enjoy it much.

Harold has a bad hand. It is either badly sprained or broken. Dr. King could not tell as it was swollen so much, but he has gone back to see him this A.M. The rest are well.

With lots of love,
DAD

May 24, 1928

DEAR VERNON,

I have time this A.M. just to write a note. Mama, Roger, and I will get to Raleigh, if nothing happens, Thursday evening, and will stay at the Bland Hotel that night. Will leave with you Friday for Durham with you in our company.

I think you had better apply to Mr. Boger for work as a supply teacher for the summer, as you could not do much with band in so short a time, and then let it drop. I believe he will give you a job, though I don't know.

Hastily,
DAD

(May 26, 1928)

DEAR VERNON,

Continuing from yesterday, I will say that Marshall Weaver, who ordered the *Pathfinder,* is not getting it, but is getting the *Normal Instructor—Primary Plans* instead.

Please look into this.

DAD

---

[3]Evangelist.

Letters Addressed to Vernon
While He Was a Student
at
the University of North Carolina

1928—1932

DEAR VERNON,

How are you feeling today after your first night within the confines of that historic seat of learning? What was the result of your call on Mr. Lawrence yesterday p.m.? I do hope his efforts in your behalf were successful.

We got home without any mishap at seven o'clock. Stopped in Greensboro for more than an hour and in Salisbury for a short time. Mama was feeling all right, but Roger was not very well. He did not go to school yesterday.

I am enclosing a letter I just received from Harold.[1] Please make out the list for him at once.

With love.

DAD

Friday A.M.

(Sept. 15, 1928)

MY DEAR VERNON,

We have received both of your cards, and Mama asked me to be sure and write you in reply this morning. I have just come into the schoolroom after fixing a puncture, and have only a few minutes to spare.

First, let me say that I think you should eat at least one hot meal a day. Be sure to eat enough and don't starve yourself out.

I hope it will not be long before you can get work of some sort, if not typewriting, then something else. Have you tried the boardinghouses and cafes?

If you need anything let me know.

YOUR DEVOTED DAD

Sept. 19, 1928

MY DEAR VERNON,

By the time you get this you will have become a student at the university, I presume, and it is a liberal education for a father to have a boy in college. It makes him feel proud and old and rejuvenated and foolish and dignified, et cetera. Anyway, I'm

---

[1]Harold had just entered the seventh grade at the North Carolina State School for the Blind.

happy that you are there. I'm happy that your ambition is sufficient to cause you to endure hardship for the sake of education. God bless you, boy of mine, and keep you.

I am sending you a small order for magazines. It may be a few cents in your pocket. I hope you got the other orders you spoke of. How much clear money have you made? Have you any other work in view yet?

Roger's school is out this week. He has made good progress this summer. Harold is getting along well, too. Mr. Barber saw him last week.

Hope to hear from you today.

Affectionately,
DAD

Sept. 26, 1928

MY DEAR VERNON,

Tuesday has been an outstanding day of the week in our household for a number of years because it means a letter from you. Yesterday was such a day, and we were glad to hear from you, and to know that our dreams and aspirations for you are being fulfilled. I presume you are settled down to the routine of work now, and are eating regular meals again. Are the three subjects all you are taking now?

Possibly those who advise you to stick to your typewriter as a means of making money are right, but it seems to me that anything you could get to do would help out. It is fine for Lawrence to let you use his trombone, and I hope you will get in the band and that it will not be too hard for you.

The boys and Mama have been picking cotton. Hope to get over mine the first time today. Won't make half a crop, though.

No news except the usual runaways—new boys—gossip of neighbors.

It is time for class, so will have to stop.

With love,
DAD

52

October 12, 1928

MY DEAR VERNON,

I don't know whether Mama has written to you this week or not, so I'll write a few lines while I am waiting for the boys to prepare their spelling lesson.

This has been a hectic week here. We went to the Fair Tuesday, and when we returned to the school about six o'clock, we ate supper and then the boys all wanted to go to bed, so about 7:30 I put them in and went back to the Fair. It is said that the crowds are larger than ever before.

Tonight we are to have an unusually good picture show, *Ramona.* Mr. Means is to bring it out here for us.

Certainly am glad you are getting so much work to do, I mean typing. I think it the best to bank your money and pay by check.

Elroy is picking cotton but expects to help Mr. Johnson paint his house next week. He painted my car shed last week. Roger is also picking cotton. Mama tried it one day, but broke herself down and has not been back since.

Go to church every Sunday, Son, and do right.

With love,

DAD

Oct. 23, 1928

MY DEAR SON,

I note with disappointment your low mark on French quiz. How does your mark compare with the marks of others in your class? I hope you will snap into the work of your class, and make a big success of it. You certainly do have to do a lot of writing; but that is what you hope to do in the future, isn't it? I wish you would send me a copy of "Caducities," whatever that means, for I'm anxious to see some of your work.

Should like very much to see Gimghoul, and when I go to see you, as I hope to do some time, you must take me there.

And so you don't like olives! Well, you have lots to learn yet. Your old Dad can show you a thing or two when it comes to eating olives. They are great.

53

When you got through with those circulars, I bet you were tired. You know I have to read, fold, address, and seal about 80 letters at the end of each month, and it is no mean job.

We have not heard from Harold in more than a week. They may have operated on his tonsils or eyes, as I gave my permission about two weeks ago. I sincerely hope he will be benefitted. Elroy is up in the mountains somewhere. He went home with Miss Greenlee last Saturday, and was expecting to stay a month if he could get a job up there.

We have out a bale of cotton, but has not been ginned yet.

Am enclosing your note which I paid last week. Your money came O.K.

With love,
DAD

(Oct. 31, 1928)

MY DEAR SON,

Mama and I expect to go to town after school today and I will get your cap and send it to you tomorrow. Don't send me any money for it. I will get you a pretty good one, but if you should not like it, return it, and I will make another choice. If you need anything else, let me know.

Yes, we heard from Harold a few days ago. I think he was so enthusiastic about going to the Fair that he forgot to write. He said that Mr. Johnson, who is on his vacation, called to see him while en route to Rocky Mount. We miss Harold so much. You know that while at home his tongue was hardly ever still. Now that you, Elroy, and Harold are away, home seems rather lonesome. Elroy seems to be having a fine time at Miss Greenlee's.

I knew that Grier expected to attend the Carolina-Tech game. Did you see him? I would like to see a game of football again, but I presume that my opportunities for seeing that great game have passed, since I have my vacation when football is out of season.

Sorry that you could not decipher the chemistry notes. Looks like a college man ought to write a legible hand, doesn't it? (No reflections.)

J. Clyde Turner, if I mistake not, is a Buies' Creek boy, classmate of Mama's. I have never seen him. He has a great name among Baptists and am glad you have the privilege of hearing him.

Harrisburg school starts again Monday, I think. Roger is anxious for it to commence. He has been mighty smart this fall, helping Mama and picking cotton. We expect to have his picture made today.

Did I tell you that we went to Charlotte last week to see the Vitaphone production—Al Jolson in the *Singing Fool?* It is a heart-touching show, and even better, I deem, than *The Jazz Singer,* his first play. If you ever have a chance, go see it and charge to me. It is so good I want you to see it.

Mama and I hope to go to High Point in November to attend the Baptist State Convention one day. Aunt Bert and Mr. Dunlap will be there; so will many other friends of former years, so we hope to have a very enjoyable time. We also hope to attend the protracted meeting at our church, which begins November 18.

Mr. Arch White's gin was destroyed by fire last night. Several farmers of the neighborhood lost some cotton in the fire. It is especially hard on the farmers to lose their cotton, as there is hardly a half of a crop made in this section, anyway. The only reason I did not have a bale at the gin when it was burned is because I couldn't get Mr. J. Lee to haul it yesterday.

I must tell you that I have a new blue suit. This is news. Also Mama has a new coat, and expects to get a new dress this week. Also Roger has a new suit. Also Elroy has one, but I believe he got that before you left. Another item of interest is we have the beaverboard in the hall painted. Also I have two new tires on my Ford. Also Roger had two teeth pulled last Saturday. Again, thirteen boys ran off Sunday. All but 3 are back. Another item, I lost one at the ball ground Saturday. He got to Salisbury, and is back. Another item—there goes the bell.

With love,
DAD

March 6, 1929

DEAR VERNON,

I saw a man the other day who must have suffered all his life with the disease a touch of which is now affecting you. It's a mental ailment. This man was ragged and miserable, hungry and cold, a tramp, a wanderer of the wasteland, "not content to settle down and accomplish something." However, he evidently was not college bred. A college education is not necessary for that kind of life.

I know a man in Sanford who *is* college bred. He has two or three medals and a title or two. He has license to practice law and he makes baskets and mends doorsteps for a living.

Now, you don't need a doctor at all. You may outgrow it. You will outgrow it unless you are *non compos mentis*. Life is not uninteresting, that is, a life of service is not. I've had my ups and downs, but through it all I have retained a firm belief in the goodness of God, I have kept a zest for life, and I have the capacity to enjoy and so I think the world's all right.

Mama will write the news, if any. I love you.

DAD

(April 12, 1929)

DEAR VERNON,

I don't know whether or not Mama has written to you this week, so I will write a letter anyway.

Am glad you have decided to attend summer school. I think you can make enough to pay expenses, but if not, call on me and I will help you out.

So you are still having to wage war on math. Well, Bill Jones says "it is not the size of the dog in the fight, but the size of the fight in the dog that counts."

Commencement is on at Harrisburg. Mama and I went Wednesday night. Tonight the junior play will be presented. We may go.

Elroy does not improve very fast, though I think he is getting some better.[1] I fear that he will never be entirely over it, but he

---

[1]From rheumatic fever.

may recover and never be bothered with it again.

Mama and I have planned to go to Washington when I get my vacation, but unless Elroy gets much better we can't go.

Our home is a much brighter place since we have electric lights.

With love,
DAD

(May 10, 1929)

DEAR VERNON,

I have just got back from town after having consulted "Dr." Porter about my bronchitis. He gave me some medicine which I hope will relieve me some. My bronchitis is very bad when I have a cold, as I do now, and gets me so stopped up I can't sleep much. After writing you and Harold a note, think I will lie down and try to get a nap.

Elroy is improving slowly. He hopes to be well enough to go to Aunt Laura's to stay while Mama and I are in Washington—if I get able to make the trip. Roger will stay at Walter's in Durham. If nothing happens we will pass Chapel Hill about 10 o'clock Wednesday morning, May 15. If you could get excused from class for a few minutes and meet us at Post Office, we would like to see you for a short time. We won't have long to stay, as we want to stop in Durham and Raleigh and then get halfway to Washington before night.

Mama certainly appreciated the Mother's Day card.

Nearly mail time.

DAD

Tuesday Morning
(May 22, 1929)

DEAR VERNON,

Since returning from our trip to Washington, Mama and I have been very busy, and rather tired. She has not been very well either, and I, of course, have foot trouble, but am in school. We certainly had a wonderful trip. Among the places visited were the Monument, the White House, the Capitol, the Zoo, Arlington, Mt.

Vernon, Congressional Library, the Pan-American Building, the Army and Navy Building and many other places in Washington, and the Luray Caverns and the Natural Bridge in Virginia.

Elroy seems much better. I hope he will soon be able to get around all right.

Harold comes home Friday. Will be glad to have him at home.

Miss Elva Rosser is to come to our house Wednesday and spend a few days. She is a fine woman.

Hope to hear from you today. Mail time now.

DAD

Tuesday A.M.
(June 18, 1929)

MY DEAR VERNON,

Your letter came Sunday and, as usual, we were glad to hear from you. You certainly did make good time on your way back to school. I was afraid that since it was so early you might have to wait some time in Salisbury before getting a ride.

I hope that you will not have to pay tuition, but if you do and if you don't have the money let me know, and I will help you.

Mama and I drove over to see our lot in Charlotte Sunday. It is a very pretty place and may be valuable some day. On our way back we stopped at West Lake Park for a few minutes. Our place is not far from the park.

Roy Ritchie is married. He has been married since Nov. and they kept it a secret until yesterday.

A new house is being built at the Carpenter place. It belongs to a Mr. Billings of Concord.

We went to Kannapolis Wednesday night and again Friday night to hear Dr. Little, who is holding a meeting there. He is such a friendly man and is really a man of God. We may go again tomorrow night.

With love,
DAD

Monday, July 8, '29

DEAR VERNON,

The feathered biped of diminuitive proportions, which we had had incarcerated for several days, escaped the executioner's ax Saturday. Upon the receipt of your card he—or she, I do not know the gender—was granted a reprieve of indefinite duration. I regretted the necessity granting the reprieve, but without you to assist in the last sad rites over his—or shis—remains, the execution would have been rather barbaric, since the victim is so young. We will look forward to your presence at some future decapitation of the same fowl.

Mama and I went to the union meeting on the lawn at the "Y" last night. Enjoyed it very much. Instead of meeting in the various churches for evening worship the united congregations assemble for the month of July in one body. I like the plan.

Did we tell you that we spent Sunday evening of last week at Badin? Mr. and Mrs. Teague, Mrs. Conley, and Miss Greenlee went with us. We had a good time.

With love,
DAD

July 18, 1929

DEAR VERNON,

While I am waiting for breakfast I will write you a note. It is only six o'clock, and I imagine you are still in bed. This being Thursday and my week on duty, I left the ford (notice little "f") at home so that Elroy can bring the folks to the picture show tonight . . . .

I went to a peach orchard beyond Harrisburg yesterday and bought two bushels of peaches. They are very poor peaches, but, as they were the best in the neighborhood, I bought them. Mama was at work canning them when I left home this morning.

I hope you will get to come home some time soon.

It is about time for me to get to shaving if I do it before breakfast.

With love,
DAD

Aug. 6th (1929)

Dear Son,

I know that it has been hard on you to be so closely confined during the very hot weather we have had; but yesterday and today have been rather pleasant, for which I am thankful. As you know, I, too, am shut up for most of the day, and some of my boys, the companions of my incarceration, have extensively odoriferous pedal extremities which make the atmosphere of my schoolroom none too pleasant.

I hope the pains around your heart have ceased by now. If not, I would advise you to see the best Dr. you can get to, and see if he can help you. You must take good care of yourself. Have you ever consulted the Dr. there?

For some time I have been taking treatment under King for thyroid trouble. Sooner or later I expect that I will have to undergo an operation, but it scares me to think of it. But if goitre develops I will have to.

Elroy is at Miss Greenlee's. Seems to be having a good time. The Dr. has not finished Harold's teeth yet. He spent from Sunday until Thursday at the Whites'. While he was away, Liverman came to see him.

The boys are out in the yard eating melon. If I get away, I will have to beat it, and since I am so nervous I can't write, I'll just stop.

With love,
Dad

Mama and I hope to go to the Brooks reunion at Jonesboro Saturday.

(Oct. 25, 1929)

Dear Vernon,

Mama and I went to see Harold Monday. He is not getting along well at all, and it grieves me very much. I hope that he will try to improve and I believe he will. Mr. Lineberry was not there, but I talked with Mr. Griffin. He and Miss Holmes said that Dr. Hicks would operate on his eyes this week or next, and if his sight is improved, as I hope it will be, I will take him home. I think

Harold dislikes the place and since he can't read with his fingers very well and, since his sight is really too poor to read with his eyes, he doesn't want to stay. He is not dumb at all, but is not inclined to put out as he should.

We certainly had a rainy time coming home Monday night. I didn't know but what any moment would be the last, as the rain was blinding. Wish we could have come by to see you, but did not have a minute to spare.

Thank you for the paper.

With love,
DAD

November 7, 1929

DEAR VERNON,

Mama wrote to Harold last night and asked me to write to you today. She is a better letter writer than I am, so you see you are not getting a square deal.

Your letters are always interesting—and short. If this of mine is not the former, it will certainly be the latter since I know nothing much to say. Elroy and Harold[1] are both going to school. Elroy is starting with more enthusiasm than he has ever evinced before. Last night at ten o'clock he was still working on his lessons. Roger, too, seems to be getting along nicely in school. We had a letter from Harold Tuesday. He had not had his operation when he wrote but was having drops put in his eyes preparatory to the operation. I do hope it will benefit his eyes.

Last Saturday I paid a man in Charlotte ten dollars more than was due him, and didn't discover my mistake until I got home. I immediately went back and, after quite an argument, won my case. I didn't much expect to get my eagle back, but did.

How are you making out for money? Keep plenty of work?

It is time for class.

With love,
DAD

---

[1] "Roger" was intended.

Nov. 20, 1929

DEAR VERNON,

I am glad that Mr. Grant's successor has retained you in his office. That, I take it, means that your work is efficient, as Al Smith says. (Excuse these blots which my leaky pen has just made.)

Do you think you will come home Christmas and Thanksgiving? I hope you can come. I want to see you.

Mama is not very well today. She woke up with the headache. As for a Christmas present for her, I would suggest a pair of stockings, a pair of gloves—no don't get gloves as I will get them—or a dish of some kind. Some kind of a pin for her dress—brooch I believe they call 'em, a ring for her finger, or a book to read would be nice. Then, 3½ yards of some dress goods would about make her a frock, and I think an overshoe for each of her little feet would be useful. A box of stationery, an electric table lamp, or curling irons are needed.

Now won't you suggest something for my son who is away at the university?

DAD

Dec. 6, 1929

DEAR VERNON,

I am at work, but am not at all well. Got no strength, and not much appetite. Guess I will be all right before long. Mama has sore throat and cold this A.M. I trust she is not taking whatever it was I had.

Elroy's report for the past month was pretty good. He did not even make a conditional failure, and that is good for one who doesn't like school.

I think you would do pretty well to sell your radio for $20.00 if you can still get that for it. Tubes will cost you at least $5 at Kresses, B batteries will cost you $3 at same place, and a storage battery will cost $7 or $8. I have a good loudspeaker—Magnavox—which you can have. By giving said speaker you might get $25 or $30 for it. If you want the speaker, let me know.

With love,
DAD

March 5, 1930

DEAR VERNON,

It has been a long time since I have written you, so if you can do without a letter from Mama this week, I'll try to pass on to you whatever news I can think of. In the first place, my health is better than it has been for some time. I believe I am gaining some of my lost avoirdupois and regaining an appetite.

Mama (this is item no. 2) has been suffering with rheumatism for several days. I don't know whether it is due to the fact that she wears false teeth.

Thirdly, Harold,[1] who never started in algebra until 3 weeks ago, after the others of his class had passed on to equations, made 92 on exam yesterday. Only one made a higher mark. I am proud of his progress.

I am glad that you are coming home soon. Seems like a long time since I saw you.

I don't know whether Mama told you that I won two tickets to the theater, and two dollars in money not long ago. It was a cartoon ad contest in *Tribune*. Now if I can win another this week, I will be glad. Sometime when I can get hold of the money, I will get you to order me a dictionary.

I'll try to get Mama to tell the rest as I am out of news.

DAD

April 23, 1930

DEAR VERNON,

We were glad to get your letter yesterday. When, as a few weeks ago, Tuesday does not bring us a letter from you, we feel somehow that we've missed payday or something.

We, too, were on the go all day Sunday, but we traveled a la Ford. Sunday morning we went to Sunday School and church at Concord. Our pastor, Mr. Summers, whom we like mighty well, preached an excellent sermon, but, in my estimation, his discourse that morning was not so good as his sermon Sunday evening, when he preached on forgiveness. In the afternoon we took Aunt Emma Eagle to Salisbury to put some flowers on Ernest Fetzer's grave.

---

[1]Back at home and in school at Harrisburg.

Yes, we are very happy that you were on the honor roll last quarter.

Did Mama tell you that George Lawrence spent a night at J.T.S. last week? I was delighted to see the fellow. What he told me about you pleased me very much.

Now, don't you send me any money. I've had my teeth pulled—that is, all that need to be out—and I have only one to be filled. He will wait for his pay until next month, so I don't need your help. (Gracious, that sounds sorter uppish, or something, doesn't it?) Anyway, I mean to say I want you to save your money until you get a vacation, then spend some of it having a good time and going to places that interest you.

Well it's 9:00 o'clock. *Tempus Fugit,* as Harold says. But I've never been able to time flies as they go so fast. Just an item or two more.

Mama and boys go to Harrisburg to a play tonight. Roger is in the play.

Fred Bost's house was damaged some $2,000 worth by fire Sunday.

DAD

Wednesday A.M.
(May 14, 1930)

DEAR VERNON,

We were sorry that you could not come home last week. Hope it won't be long until you can come. I guess you enjoyed your trip to Raleigh. Harold got back Sunday afternoon and says that he had a very good time.

I have never looked through a telescope of any great magnitude. It must be interesting to look at the stars and the moon and the great expanse of the heavens through a telescope. Even when seeing these wonders with the naked eye the psalmist was constrained to cry out "When I consider thy heavens, the work of thy fingers, the moon and the stars, which thou has ordained; What is man, that thou art mindful of him?"

Did you enjoy your visit to Prof. Williams's?

I don't know for sure, but it is my hope that I will get my vacation in June. We are not planning any big trips this year as money is very scarce. We hope to visit Mama's people and you. Then, I think a few days idling at home and a few days work in Elroy's cotton field will use up my vacation very happily, even if I have no money to spend.

I bought a mule, aged and gray, only she's red, poor, and hungry, for Elroy to work. He has five acres in cotton and expects to plant three in corn. Planted watermelons yesterday.

Harold is bottoming some chairs.

Roger reads. Mama works. I quit.

DAD

May 22 (1930)

DEAR VERNON,

Last Thursday evening we saw Buster Keaton in *Steamboat Bill.* Buster played the part of a young collegian. He might have been one of your human machines, a mere automaton, that, so far as his spiritual or emotional nature, or his will power, or his common sense is concerned, would furnish as alter ego for a lot of the fellows in college. I might add that he looked collegiate, too. What man, made in the image of God, crowned with glory, redeemed from destruction, saved by grace, would exchange his life, even with its hunger, its fatigue, its loves, its hopes, for the existence of one of your monkeys on a string? Give me the chance to live and labor and suffer and love and hope and hunger, knowing that the path I travel leads not *to* the graveyard, but *through* the graveyard, home.

With love,
DAD

Sept. 19, 1930

DEAR VERNON,

Mr. Godown returned last night from New Jersey, where he went to attend the burial of his step-father.

The Stroupes have moved to Concord, much to Harold's regret. Revis is in school at China Grove.

School at Harrisburg closed last week.

Mama attended a meeting of her Sunday School class at the home of Mrs. L. R. Crooks on McGill St. last night.

The picture at the training school last night was *Salute.*

Frank Lisk went to New York while on his vacation. He has not returned to the school yet.

My cotton is opening, but at 10¢ a pound I will lose money.

Harold finished his chairs yesterday.

John Russel is spending his vacation in Florida.

Mrs. Haden Talbert was baptized by Bro. Summers Sunday night.

Mr. Willis Stallings died last night.

Our Fair will begin Oct. 14.

Haden will be on jury duty during fair week, so I'll be on duty here. Sorry.

Mr. Thompson is spending his vacation at Chase City, Va.

I have read several of Horace's odes. They are not so hard.

We have a new teacher—a Mr. Wingate, graduate of Duke last year. Nice boy.

I'm sitting on a boil. It hurts.

Scarborough returned last week from Carolina beach.

I had a letter from Uncle Ike yesterday. He just wanted to thank me again for the arrowhead screen.

An old lady—Mrs. Barrier—was killed by an automobile in Concord Saturday night.

The political pot is boiling. Lee White is a candidate for county commissioner.

Harold bought himself a new pair of shoes yesterday.

Glad you made so much addressing envelopes.

I love you.

DAD

Thursday P.M. Oct. 30 '30

DEAR VERNON,

I deposited your money at noon today. Herewith is receipt and checkbook. The bank, I presume, is sound.

A Vitaphone is being installed in our auditorium, whether just on trial or whether for keeps I don't know. It will do its stuff for us tonight. Am looking forward to it with pleasure.

Mama entered some flowers at the flower show in Concord today. They were very pretty, and I hope she wins one of the prizes, though she says her exhibit is not as good as several others.

Hurriedly,
DAD

Monday A.M.
(Dec. 8, 1930)
DEAR VERNON,

I wonder if you got back to Chapel Hill without any trouble Sunday afternoon? I did not get to see Jno. Rogers as he was gone when I got back to Sanford. We got home about 8 o'clock. Had a nice drive in the rain.

Elroy is making expenses and enough for payment on his Ford. His business is picking up some. Harold didn't get back until Monday morning.

The boys at the school are very restless. Five ran off last night and eight Friday. All back but four.

Vernon, I need to borrow some money. If you can lend me $20 until Feb. 1st I would appreciate it. However, if you can't spare it, it will be all right as I can borrow it from Tom Greer, I think. I owe a few little debts—Dr. King $5, drugstore $7.50, Reid Motor Co. $5, which I want to pay before Christmas, and I must pay my fire insurance and get the license for the Ford. If you can lend me $20, please send me a check at once. As I said before, if you can't spare it, it will be absolutely all right. I hate to ask you.

With love,
DAD

(Jan., 1931)
DEAR VERNON,

Your letter and the check reached me yesterday. Many thanks. If you should need it before Feb., just let me know and I will remit.

We also received your other letter. Glad you got back all right. After I left you I was afraid it was going to rain, and I had about decided to go back and take you on when it stopped raining.

Harold made three A's and a B on his last exams at Harrisburg, and algebra still to hear from. He seems to be getting along well.

This is National Golden Rule Week, and I hope to live in accordance to that rule not only this week but all the weeks to come to a greater extent than I have in the past.

With love,
DAD

(Jan. 13, 1931)

DEAR VERNON,

The enclosed letter from Mama was written last week and has been safely cared for in my pocket ever since.

I received your letter yesterday. Godown has some negatives which he said I could borrow, and as soon as I get them (which will be whenever he takes a notion to look for them) I will mail them to you, or have some developed and send the pictures if you prefer. He wants to get the negatives back.

I am enclosing pictures of our Thanksgiving rabbit hunt. They are Mr. Johnson's.

Elroy has at last got out of the News mess. That experiment cost me $80.00.

Hastily,
DAD

Your name was in *Observer.* Congratulations.

Feb. 1st, 1931

DEAR VERNON,

Herewith is ck. for $20. I do thank you so much for the loan. If it had not been for that, I don't know how I would have made out.

I had a letter from Mr. Hobbs last week. He expressed the highest pleasure in your good work there (what a bunglesome way I put this sentence) and congratulated *me.* I am to be congratulated for having such a son, but for his success I deserve nothing.

For some time now I have not been able to sleep at night much. I stayed up until after three last night. I went to town at dinner time and got Dr. Porter to give me something to make me sleep.

With love,
DAD

April 10, 1931

DEAR VERNON,

This letter should have been written this morning so that you could have gotten it tomorrow, but I couldn't get it done. However, as I have nothing important to say, I presume it will make no difference if my letter is a day late.

From the amount of work you are having to do, I don't see that you would have much time for outside work. You must be on the go all the time.

Isn't your present boarding place a little cheaper than some of the places at which you have eaten?

My eye is better. I have to go back to Salisbury at least once more, but I hope once is all. Am afraid to ask what I owe him.

Miss Hartsell has not come back to work yet. She has been out over a month. She hopes to be able to come back next week.

Niblock got the contract to rebuild the burned cottages. He started to work on them yesterday.

Sold old Ford for $12.50 *on time.* Don't know when I'll get the money for it, if ever.

Affectionately,
DAD

Wednesday A.M.
(May 6, 1931)

DEAR VERNON,

As is always the case, we were glad to get your letter yesterday. Your comprehensive examination was indeed comprehensive. I hope you passed it all right.

I know you are glad to have a chance to make some money again. Don't work too hard. You know if you need more than you will have, I will get it for you some way.

My eye is not well, but doesn't bother me very much. It may never be much better than it is, though, since it is so much better than it was, I am thankful.

I ordered some oval pith for Harold last week. Hope he can get a good many chairs to do this summer. He counts on going to Raleigh for the picnic.

We are having a good meeting at our church. Mr. Summers, assisted by Rev. Mr. Lee, from Raleigh is conducting the meeting. I was very happy to see Roger join the church.

Vernon, if you should happen to have a declamation suitable for sixth graders I would be glad to borrow it for a contest speech for the Barnhardt Prize. The contest will be July 4.

I don't know when I will get my vacation. I asked for it in June, but it is uncertain whether I can get it then.

With love,
DAD

May 15, 1931

DEAR VERNON,

While waiting for my boys to prepare their English lessons, I'll write you a note. We were glad to hear that you did so well with your work last week. I know you must have been kept busy. Your success makes us happy.

I presume you read of the tragedy at Mt. Pleasant last week. It has created a lot of excitement around here. The man Barrier was 1st cousin of Lee Ritchie's. The women were buried yesterday.

It is uncertain when I will get my vacation. I had hoped to have it in June, but I am not at all sure I can get it then, as there are two or three others that applied for that month before I did. I don't suppose I will be able to go anywhere much, anyway, but just to get away from this school for a while will be a pleasure.

Dr. Brawley has at last turned me loose, unless my eye gets worse again. Don't know what my bill will be. I asked him Monday, and he said, "Oh, not much." I hope he meant it.

When will you be home again? Seems like it has been a long time since I have seen you.

If I were not in such a hurry, you could read this writing with more ease.

But my time is out, so now for nouns, verbs, and such junk.

Anyway, I have no other styles of penmanship.[1]

DAD

(May 21, 1931)

DEAR VERNON,

I was told by Mr. Fisher that my vacation will start just as soon as Johnson gets back. He will be away until the 20 of June, so I suppose mine will begin then. When does yours come? How long will you have before summer school starts?

Wish I could attend the Playmaker production, but I am on cottage duty and can't get off. On account of sickness I will have to count off 11 days from my vacation period, and that leaves only 19. So I had better not lose any more time before June 20 if I can help it.

Mama has a right bad cold. It's the first she has had in a year or more. The rest are well. Excuse this note.

DAD

May 27, 1931

MY DEAR VERNON,

I think Mama is writing to you this morning too, but what I saw in today's paper calls for a few remarks from me.

Congratulations, felicitations, and attaboy! At—, I repeat with all the emphasis I can command, -taboy!

If you don't know what it's all about, I'll tell you that I'm happy that you are one of the 343 fellows who, by their outstanding work there, has won an award. What was it?

DAD

_____

[1]The last three sentences were in three different styles of penmanship.

Friday A.M.
(July 10, 1931)

Dear Vernon,

I don't know whether you have been "written to" since we came home or not, so I'll just scribble a few lines while my English class tries to learn something about adjectives.

After leaving you last week, we went to Jonesboro and visited the Yarboros. Saturday, Will Y. and I went to Fayetteville. Saturday night we stayed at Mrs. Oehler's (Mae Barnes') and Sunday night at Ike Dunlap's. Thoroughly enjoyed my vacation.

Elroy and Harold got along very nicely. They had company nearly every night, Mr. Summers's boy, and Pressler's boy from Concord.

Mama is canning blackberries. There are lots of them this year. Garden about dried up by dry weather. (Now that's a great sentence, isn't it?)

Would like to be there for the Playmakers. Can't.

Dad

(Sept. 3, 1931)

Dear Vernon,

We received your box Monday. Interment of the lamented little black took place at sunset yesterday. Cactus doing very well. Pigs are accepting their new quarters, but don't seem to appreciate being incarcerated. Elroy driving bread truck a few days this week. Mama O.K. And so am I except for a cold, sinus trouble, a corn on the elbow, a fretful disposition, and a flat pocketbook. Tolerably long.

Dad

October 1, 1931

Dear Vernon,

Now that I have a few minutes to spare in the schoolroom before beginning with my regular work, I will write to you. Have got my reports all finished, boys' letters off, and everything ready for another month of grinding.

I imagine addressing envelopes has become quite a monotonous task to you. How many did you address in Sept.? Do you find time to do your schoolwork? From the cost of your books, you must have plenty to keep you going night and day.

Say, do you know Johnnie Branch? I think he is a former training school boy, AWOL. I would like to know for sure, if you can tell me. The one we had was from Rhodiss, but I think his people moved somewhere, maybe to Salisbury.

Now for the news events of the week. Elroy is driving a bread truck from Gastonia to Shelby and adjacent towns. Think he makes about $15.00 per week. Roger has had red eyes for a week or so, so Mama and I took him to see Dr. Brawley. He says there is nothing serious the matter, and gave some medicine to relieve the inflammation. Said his lens are O.K.

Mama is very well, and so am I. Roger is to have a birthday party the 5th and expects his Sunday School class to be present.

Mama and I went to see *Monkey Business* at Concord Theater Tuesday night. We were the guests of Miss Greenlee. Other members of the party were Mrs. Conley, Mrs. Haywood, and Mrs. (Dr.) Smoot. The play was rather funny.

There is a case of scarlet fever here at the school. It may mean that we will not have to take the boys to the Fair this year. The Fair starts the 14th, I think.

Tom Grier is back from Canada and today resumed his work at the school. I am glad for him to be back on the job again.

Wingate has resigned and has secured work in the Navy Department in Washington as typist.

How would you like a year or so in Washington, after you get through there, doing secretarial work for Cam Morrison? You might like the experience and I believe you could get the job.

With love,
DAD

Nov. 5, 1931

DEAR VERNON,

O Mores! O Tempora! Tempus has *fugit* some more! The Fair has passed, Halloween is but a memory and it's only three weeks until Thanksgiving. Soon 1931 will be over, soon my working days will be over, soon I will be over. But it has been, and still is, a lot of fun to carry on. The more I read the newspapers, and history, and Will Rogers, and the Hotel Stenographer, and Little Orphan Annie, the more they convince me that there is no place in the world that has a denser population—from the shoulders up—than wherever people live. So, I repeat, *O Tempora!*

Dr. Rowan is in the hospital for the insane, Al Capone is in prison, and I'm in debt. I'm better off than they.

Mama has a new coat, Roger has a picnic with his Sunday School class tonight on the big rock, and I have a class ready to recite.

Now, if you know what it's all about, you should be able to read Sanskrit. I've got a dark brown taste in my mouth and need a pill, I guess.

With love,

DAD

P.S. I can't get this folded to fit, so maybe I'll not send it.

Dec. 9, 1931

DEAR VERNON,

I don't know a thing to write, but as Mama has been quilting all day for two days, she asked me to write to you tonight, so like an obedient husband and father, I take my pencil in hand to do as I was bid—or bidden.

Sorry you are having so much trouble getting your play across. I hope your cast will now stay put, and that it—the play—will go over big. I would like to see it produced.

Back to the fact that Mama has been quilting—Mrs. Conley has been helping her, and Mrs. Horton, too. Mrs. Conley has much to say about the immense size of said quilts, but I'm a whale of a man (physically) and when I'm well-covered up, I'm well-covered up.

How long did you have to wait before Walker picked you up? It must not have been very long, from what he said.

Mr. Frank Pharr is very low. He has not been conscious since he fell last week. It is not thought that he will ever get well.

I bought a cord of slabs yesterday. Three dollars.

I bought a gallon[1] of gasoline yesterday. Two dollars and fifty cents.

I ate dinner at second cottage today. Potato pie and pigs in a blanket.

I came home tonight with a bad cold. Cut a turn of stove wood. Feel better.

I want to put my feet on footstool. Black cat objects. So like a nice man, I let the cat have it.

I wonder how I would feel to lie down on the big rock in the rain and sleep tonight and stay there till found tomorrow or the next day or some time. I like it here by the nice warm stove better. I'll stay here.

"All the world's a stage." "All is vanity," saith the preacher. I must stop as it would not be in good taste to write on the other side.

With love,
DAD

---

[1]In all probability he meant *tank* rather rather *gallon*.

Letters Addressed to Vernon
While He Was Working
in
Chapel Hill, North Carolina

1932—1938

Dear Vernon,

I don't know whether Mama has written you since you left or not, so I will jot down a few items myself.

Glad you suffered no ill effects from your trip back. I was uneasy about you as it was so cold. We are still in the grip of flu here at the school, but none of the cases very severe. However, there have been several deaths in Concord from it. Mama, I am afraid, is taking it. She has a cold and aches all over. I am going down to see how she is directly. I am feeling fine myself.

How do you like having a room all by yourself? Does it cost you more?

I plan to go to Charlotte tomorrow and return my Sears battery that I bought a month ago. It has gone bad already.

A good many of the boys have gone home this month, and among them my thorn in the flesh, Rufus Brown from High Point.

School will resume at Harrisburg Monday. The roads in the county have been so bad that buses could not travel them, and so many had flu that there was no school this week.

With love,
Dad

Jan. 21, 1932

Dear Vernon,

I had an egg for breakfast. When I don't have an egg for breakfast—that is when I eat breakfast at the school—I feel that my breakfast has not been a very good breakfast. Mama spent the afternoon yesterday with Mrs. Conley. Mrs. Conley spent the afternoon day before yesterday. I have just been interrupted by Mr. Pool coming into my room to select a basketball team. One of the boys he picked out is *non compos mentis*. He says if he doesn't use his head very much it will last longer. My salary was cut another ten dollars recently. Don't know how, but I'll get along some way. A Mr. DeHart has moved into Hayden's house. He is running the Whit Pharr—Lee White dispensary of gasoline. Grady is driving a candy truck for Covington. I have been interrupted again. This time to administer punishment to a boy who befouled the atmosphere of the room. Hope I get a chance to vote for Daniels for governor. Have you got your M.A. play going yet? It is enough to make one cross to try to shave when you have no hot water, no sharp razor, no Colgate's soap (only Williams's, which you can buy for 3¢ a cake at Penny's), and when your face is chapped. Harold is getting along well in school. He is very popular in Concord. Mr. Johnson is very much "put out" with his small salary. He makes only $90. Have just (wrong pen) been interrupted again; this time by Godown who wants to know who said of Washington that he was "first in war, first in peace, etc." I don't know. Do you? Time's up.

With love,
DAD

(Feb. 11, 1932)

DEAR VERNON,

I know a poor fellow named Crook
Who cracked his brain when he undertook
   To write a queer story
   Fantastic and gory,
So now he is demented, Gadzook!

Anyway it's a curious, "Poe-etic" story. I wish you would send some more of your contributions to the *Carolina Magazine*. Mrs. Duckett, who read your "Butler Screams," just came in and told me to tell you that last night, after reading your piece, she had a horrifying dream about having been found alive.

I don't know what Audible Light is—what is it?

The Kings Daughters are to be out here tomorrow afternoon and give some sort of program. I think they are going to give the boys some games. They usually tell them what noble boys they are, and that the chances for them to become presidents, governors, and judges are excellent. I don't think there are a great many here who will ever occupy those exalted positions.

Again we have as neighbors in Haden's house some undesirables. This time it is drink. One of the men was arrested Sunday for driving while drunk.

Gertrude Ferrill spent Saturday night and Sunday with us. She was sent to Charlotte by her employers in Raleigh, the Commercial Credit Co., to take a two-weeks course in some phase of their work. We took her back to Charlotte Sunday evening and attended church in the city. To see a big church like that simply packed with people, eager to listen to Dr. Little's simple gospel message, is encouraging. It shows that people are still interested in the worship of God and in things spiritual.

With love,

DAD

Feb. 25, 1932

DEAR VERNON,

For a few minutes, while the boys are preparing a geography lesson, I will see if I can guide this pen into producing legible characters on a sheet of paper, though where the thoughts are to come from I haven't the ghost of an idea, as the general spirit of discontent and nervousness which pervades this place, and which has Hayden Talbert and Bob Sappenfield laid up for a week now, has affected my mind—if any. Now that opening sentence discourages me! Ain't it sumpen? But two facts in it need elucidation: Hayden has been advised by his physician to lay off his job here for a month or so on account of his severe nervousness, Bob has had the same orders, and I am very well. But unless there is an improvement in the morale of this place we may all go bughouse soon. Really, it's a mess. But through it all I try to maintain the even tenor of my way.

Mabel Yarboro is to spend the week end with us. She is coming Saturday with one of her Meredith friends. Mr. and Mrs. Frasier spent Sunday with us two weeks ago.

The swine have been slain.

The cat will kitten in the near future.

I will send you another deposit slip next week.

The Chinese seem to be hard for the Japanese to handle.

And so long until next week.

DAD

April 7, 1932

Dear Vernon,

We were glad to get your letter Tuesday. As Mama is going to iron today, I will write to you in her stead; so, you need not look for as interesting a letter as she writes.

Glad you are making progress with your play. I know it must be a task to get it in shape. I received your report a few days before your letter came. We are very happy to get such splendid reports.

Last Saturday Mrs. Vance, from Concord, Mrs. Slack, from Kannapolis, Mrs. Conley, Mama, Roger, and I piled into my ford (or Ford) and went to Mooresville. We took a big picnic dinner of ham, eggs, tomatoes, lettuce, cake, pickles, pies, and ice tea. We all "unlaxed" and had a big time. While in Mooresville we went to see Miss Hartsell and Miss Goodman.

Cannon Mfg. Co. has given the school an old disc-type talking picture machine. I don't know how good it is, as it has not been tried out yet.

Mr. Thompson, our baker, is expecting to leave the school soon. He has bought a cafe in Kannapolis, I hear.

Mrs. Hudson, near White Hall School, died last week. I guess Mama wrote you about the death of Dr. Grier.

Elroy informs me that Clyde Hudson has been arrested for the murder of Jack Dees some time ago. Clyde is a nephew of old man Bob.

The Elwood Johnson who is under arrest as a member of the bandit gang that shot the Carolina boy is one of our old training school boys. He was sent here from Sanford.

Well, this isn't much of a letter, but with this message from Mama, "Tell him I love him," in which I join, I'll say

Goodbye,
Dad

April 21, 1932

Dear Vernon,

Hopes and ambitions, like the best laid plans of mice and men, often go fluey. But, due to the resilience of youth, it never halts progress for rebuffs to come. To the old thwarted plans never prove fatal either, for they have had so many hard knocks that it has become a matter of habit for them to grunt when they are bowled over, and then to pick themselves up, rub liniment on their joints, and try again. Anyway, I am sorry about your play. But I know you will succeed yet.

And speaking of rubbing liniment on your joints, I've been having to do just that for several days. And thereby hangs a tale. Sunday I stopped the Wreck of the Hesperus on the hill near eleventh cottage and, leaving the motor running, I started into the cottage to get my mail. When I had got almost to the cottage I noticed that the Ford, drat it, had broken loose from its mooring and was making rapid headway towards a steep incline and a three-foot ditch. I managed to board the derelict, tho' in doing so I was thrown with some violence against the frame of the posthole, wrenching my knee. But I stopped the runaway just in time. My knee, my whole leg—thigh, shin, calf, ankle, with all appurtenances belonging thereto, is swollen and painful.

Mirabile dictu, Harold made such good grades on geometry and history that on those subjects he is exempted from examination.

I will try to get Mama to write the news, if any.

With love,
DAD

April 27, 1932

DEAR VERNON,

I know so little to say this time that I had about as well not start; but maybe when I get going some thoughts will come into being. I will say first that I am glad your play is progressing. Wish I could be present at its production, and if it were not for the fact that I am jealously guarding my few days vacation (just eight days) I would go to it.

This is my week off duty but somehow it is slipping by without any very important happenings. Mama is not very well, and that always affects me as you say my knee affects yours. My knee, by the way, is better. So's the Ford. I don't want ever to become a chronic grouch, but what with a bad cold, a sore knee, a septic tank that won't work, and a schoolroom full of boys that won't either, 160 letters to read, reports to fill out, and the wolf to be beaten from the door, I feel like the Ancient Mariner, or that Shylock was going to exact his pound of flesh from me.

Mama wants to know if you will have to pay that man to present your play?

I bought two cords of wood yesterday from Mr. Will Jack Alexander. It cost me only $5.00. That is the cheapest I have bought wood in a long time. If I had time I would enjoy sawing it for the stove.

As I sit here in my chair (with one of the rockers broken) I am enjoying a concert by the U.S. Marine Band over the radio. "Down South" is being played now, and it is a favorite of mine.

We got back in the church Sunday. The organ, the carpet, and the new paint make it seem like a different place. I never had seen the church packed full until last Sunday at the night service.

Well, with the words I've said so often, "I love you, Son," I'll stop.

DAD

July 27, 1932

DEAR VERNON,

Your prospects are indeed bright. I am very glad. When do you suppose the new magazine will get started? What will you have to do if you land the job with the News Bureau? Meanwhile, I hope you may continue to get some typing to do. Have you heard from the story you sent to *American Mercury*?

Our meeting came to a close last evening; 14 or 16 were baptized Sunday night. We all like the Summers family very much. Our pastor will go to Kentucky next week to hold a meeting at his father's church.

Mama held the lucky ticket at an action sale of furniture at Sprotts last Saturday. The prize was a nice smoking stand, cabinet model. Saturday night she bought a bedroom suite. It is very nice.

Mr. Whit Pharr's house was burned to the ground last Friday

afternoon about 5 o'clock. Lightning, it is supposed. They saved most of the furniture, except what was upstairs.

I am certainly glad you are so comfortably housed. You need seven windows this hot weather.

With love,
DAD

(Aug., 1932)

VERNON,

Thanks for the loan. Hope to repay it soon.

Sometime, when you have time, will you please [type] two or three copies of the enclosed mess, and then tell me whether to burn it in the kitchen stove, or whether to submit it to the *State,* or *Observer* for publication. If you decide on publication, let me know how to get it done.

DAD

P.S. Would I be put in jail if I published this?

P.S. I have just been put through the 3rd degree by one Dr. or Mr. Ezell who is interviewing state employees. He says he knows you and that you have quite a reputation at Chapel Hill, being one of the best known men there.

Sept. 15, 1932

DEAR VERNON,

I don't know whether Mama has written to you this week or not, so I will drop you a line while I am waiting for the boys to prepare their lessons.

We have been hoping you could get home for a few days. But your work seems to be confining—as are most jobs now. It does seem like a long time since you were at home.

Do you still write feature articles for the papers? I have not seen one in two or three weeks with your name to it. And have you received pay for the ones that have been published?

I hope you will like your new room. The prospect of having a fire to punch ought to lend enchantment to the place. That reminds me that I've just had a grate made for our heater, and have bought a ton of coal. So, I don't think cold weather will sneak up on us this year.

Did Mama write you that we have at last had the wall built at the road in front of the house? It looks very nice. Cost about $17.

School is out for two months at Harrisburg. Roger got a job picking cotton at Mr. White's and Harold expects to pick, too.

Mama has "put up" a good deal of fruit for the winter, and the collards are nice, so we expect to have something to eat for a while anyway.

Time for geography.

With love,
DAD

Oct. 25, 1932

DEAR VERNON,

Yes, I know Will Keith, the redheaded Scotchman. He was a playmate of mine back in medieval times, and a very good friend. I also knew Vick's grandfather, Jacob Keith, and his great grandfather, a regular patriarch with a long, cascading white beard, who came from Scotland. Is Vick the redheaded boy with the crippled hand? I saw two of them when I was in Vass.

I am writing this with a new Swan 44 pen, with fine point. The pen was presented to me by a representative of the factory, Wrenn, who was one of my old J.T.S. boys ten years ago. I like very much.

Am glad you can have a fire this chilly weather. Too cold without a fire. Does the coal cost you extra? And do you have plenty of cover on your bed? Who chopped off the tops of the capital letters on your typewriter?

Our fair was a big success, they say. I did not go the day the boys went, as Simpson, Ritchie, and I were left here on police duty. But we went the next day, and having a pass to all the shows and for all the rides and to the grandstand, we had a good time. We had ten boys with us.

Miss Myrtle Thomas, Cabarrus County's new nurse, is a sister of Rob Thomas who married Mama's sister. Miss Thomas spent most of the day with us Friday. Mama visited her last week.

I am hoping to get off a couple of days in November to attend the Bapist State Convention in Charlotte. There will be many of our friends and acquaintances there.

How is your cold? I have one and a sore throat and a sprained ankle. I fell over a tub and skinned both shins and sprained my ankle and hurt my feelings elsewhere.

With love,
DAD

Jan. 18, 1933

DEAR VERNON,

It is cold here this morning—so different from the way your room was when you wrote. The thermometer is hovering around 60° in my schoolroom, and that makes it rather uncomfortable.

Does your new work add to your present salary, or is it part of your duties for the Bureau? I hope it boosts your salary considerably.

I am in the midst of recataloging the books in the library—or rather I should say making a list of them to be published in the new catalog which should be printed in February. It is a job, but I like it.

The C.W.A. is having the fill near the barn widened, roads on premises improved, buildings painted inside and out, an underpass to the ball ground dug and nightshirts made for this school. Mama may get to make some of the shirts. Elroy has been cutting wood for several days. He has registered for C.W.A. work. And I am just going to register a protest against the noise and paper wads that is (or are) making my schoolroom untenable.

DAD

Jan. 14, 1933

DEAR VERNON,

Will you please copy the "Answers to Questionnaire of January 11," for me? If you can, please make two copies, and send them to me as soon as you can conveniently. I enclose Questionnaire so that you may see what it's all about. I will remit upon receipt of bill—if I can. Anyway thank-you.

Think Mama is writing to you today, so I will just stop.

Love,
DAD

January 20, 1933

DEAR VERNON,

I received the Questionnaire in good time. Many thanks. Strange to relate, it won high praise from Mr. Boger. He was pleased especially with the neat form of it.

As with other state employees, we are facing another cut in salaries here. It may not come, but I look for it. Well, I guess we can live on less, but how?

I got some free tickets to the Pastime last week, so we had quite a party Wednesday night—Mrs. Conley, Miss Greenlee, Mrs. Haywood, Mama, Elroy, Harold, Roger, and I. We go so seldom that it was a real treat to us.

The boys are in school today, Saturday, to make up for some of the days lost on account of bad weather. I suppose it will be the usual Saturday program for some time. Harold wants to enter the Declamation contest this year. If you know of any suitable 10 or 12 minute pieces that you can recommend, I would be glad to know of them.

Please find out for me, if you can, how Berea College, Berea, Ky., ranks. Is it a standard college with full 4 year courses?

How do you like your new quarters? I hope you are pleased, and that you will have a better selection of eats. Are you keeping pretty busy? How about the new magazine?

I have no news.

Affectionately,
DAD

(Jan., 1933)

DEAR VERNON,

I heard a play over the radio last night that sticks in my mind. I'll tell you about it: Lassater, a young man of New York, was in love with Mary. He asked Mary to marry him. She informed him that she was engaged to Van Dine. Lassater was all broken up. That night his car collided with a circus truck in which was a gorilla. In the wreck, Lassater was wounded about the body, neck broken, and left in such bad shape that the eminent surgeon from Vienna who was at the hospital, and the other doctors, declared that he could not possibly live one hour. The gorilla, too, was taken to the hospital. It was wounded in the head—brains spattered—couldn't live. Eminent surgeon from Vienna experimented. Grafted or planted Lassater's good brain in good body of gorilla. The resulting monstrosity in the form of gorilla with Lassater's brain lived and got well. It could talk and see and hear and think and love and hate and had all the sensibilities of Lassater, but gorilla body. It being rich, spurned showman's offer of $100 per week. But when it left hospital of course no one knew the gorilla monster for Lassater. It was chased out of cafes, hotels, and everywhere. Desperate for food and a place to sleep, accepted showman's offer. Traveled with show several months. Heard over the radio of the wedding of his Mary and Van Dine. He returned to New York, hunted up the surgeon and told him unless he again put his brain back in the body of a man he would suicide. Dr. agreed to do so at first chance. A few days later Van Dine was brought to hospital, with head crushed, in dying condition. Again Lassater's brain was transplanted—this time into the body of Van Dine, Mary's husband. Now ... you can finish this story for yourself.

My ankle, though still swollen, is not very painful. I've got shoes, hoping they will help hold my ankle when I fall over tubs of beans hereafter. May get me some shin guards, or whatever you call those things football players wear, to protect my shins from skinnings when I fall over tubs of string beans. Will also need some good leather gloves, steel lined, to protect my hands from being bruised on the gravel as I try to catch when I fall over tin tubs of strung string beans.

Mrs. Conley is on her vacation. Mrs. Johnson is our matron while Mrs. Conley is away. She, Mrs. Johnson, bought and served us a mess of oysters yesterday. They were mighty good. First I've had this year.

I have had bronchitis very bad for several days. But Dr. Porter gave me some medicine for it and I'm much better. For two or three nights I couldn't sleep, but last night I rested fine. After feeling bad, I always feel good when I feel better, er sumthin.

I hope your play will be a success. Are you writing any on your thesis? Your M.A. would be a distinction worth striving for, wouldn't it?

Well, time's up. Pity the sorrows of a poor old man who has to teach geography!

DAD

January 31, 1933

DEAR VERNON,

I shall not be able to get Harold in Berea this year, as you may see from the enclosed card. I have written to Berry, in Ga., Mars Hill, Catawba, Cumberland U., at Lebanon, Tennessee, and Campbell. $275 covers the cost at Mars Hill. Haven't heard from the other places yet. Can you figure what his necessary expenses would be at Carolina? Do you think that on account of his eyes he could get help from Stanley or the Rehabilitation fund? Harold says he can get his tuition free at Washington and Lee. They, for some reason, are making that offer to one student of Harrisburg High, and Mr. Smith, the principal, says Harold will get it if he wants it. I certainly will appreciate it if you can take matter up with Mr. Stanley, or whoever may be in charge of the rehabilitation funds and see what can be done. Do you think he would have much chance there (at Carolina) to earn?

Glad you have a radio and that you have congenial companions. What do your new quarters cost you?

Mama is going to a class meeting tonight, Roger to a weiner roast, Elroy to the store, Harold to wind the town clock and I, well, I will go to bed.

"Where the swamps swallow cows," eh! Why not where swelling swamps surreptitiously swallow snouty swine seeking succulent sustenance secreted—oh, well, carry this on ad infinitum if you wish. I'm done. Anyway your Mr. Patrick is a real easterner if he knows what a pocosin is. But if he calls a turtle a *cooter,* he's from the hills. These two tests are unfailing. Try them out on your friends sometimes—they are painless. And, too, if they are "bullaces," they have had the privilege of playing with little Negroes in their youth, but if they are "muscadines," their education has been sadly neglected.

With love,
DAD

March 18, 1933

DEAR VERNON,

Since I have red ink in my pen that I use in library,[1] I will just have to use it to write this letter. As usual, we were so glad to get your letter Tuesday and to know that during these peculiar times you are getting plenty to do. I have just read in the paper that Henry Burke says the cuts for the next quarter will be from 50% to 90%. That's a whale of a lot to lop off of a fellow's wages when its already scandalously low. However, better that than nothing.

You certainly did get a bargain in the watch. I like the Elgin very much. Mine, though only 7 jewels, keeps good time.

I have been using peroxide as a mouth wash for some time. There is so much trench mouth here that I am taking precautionary measures to prevent getting it myself, if possible. Dr. Ezzell, Jr., has been working on the teeth of the boys here for 3 weeks. Kings Daughters are paying him.

I am kept very busy. What with the schoolroom and the library, to say nothing of cottage duty, my time is well-filled—or at least filled. If I can get off, I want to go to Charlotte this P.M.

Time's up.

DAD

April 6, 1933

DEAR VERNON,

This is such a beautiful morning! It rained a little during the night, and now all outdoors looks so clean and fresh and sparkling in the sunlight. I like to live on a day like this. It fills me with

---

[1]Crook established the library at J.T.S. and served as the first librarian, voluntarily adding that to his other responsibilities.

what the psalmist must have felt when he said: "What is man, that thou art mindful of him?" Since I can't get away and go fishing, or cut stove wood, or write a book, or plow the garden, I will just try to get all the pleasure out of doing what I have to do. And it has many bright spots. For instance, yesterday Osteen went home. He had been here nearly four years. When he came to my room to tell be goodbye, the tears were streaming down his cheeks and in a choked-up voice he thanked me for what I had done for him. I'm glad to be of help to others. Maybe, since I love everybody, I have got some ole-time religion. Anyway I'm happy.

I hope your watch will prove to be a splendid one. Maybe it just needed some little adjustment and will now function properly. My Elgin, though only seven jeweled, keeps good time.

Have you another roommate yet? Does it cost you more to have the room to yourself?

I hope you will soon get to come home for a few days. Seems like a long time since I saw you. Do you think you will be here Easter? If you do, let's go to Winston for the Moravian Easter service—if I can get excused from Sunday school.[1]

With love,
DAD

May 13, 1933

DEAR VERNON,

I don't know whether Mama has written to you this week or not, so I will spill our weekly tale of woe into your sympathetic ears.

1. My salary, as yours, has been cut an additional 25%.

2. I've got leg trouble, probably rheumatism again, or maybe it's gout.

3. Harold, playing with Query boys, got two front teeth knocked out. Cost $20.00.

4. One of Lizzie's tires gave out. New tire $4.50.

5. Chicken here ruthlessly slain by Haden Talbert's dog. Loss,

---

[1] All the boys at J.T.S. were required to attend Sunday School, and Crook taught a class during his entire career there. On a rotating basis, ministers from local churches held Sunday afternoon services at the school.

an egg a day till fall and a dish of chicken and dumplings next winter.

6. Black cat in poor health. May have to call veterinarian, 'er sumthin.

7. Birds ate our cherries. Hope they choke.

8. Going to Charlotte today for new suit to replace present threadbare habiliments. Cost $10.00.

9. Ate supper at home last night. Menu—4 lbs crokers. Cafe noir. Corn bread. Cost 25¢.

10. And so on, ad infinitum. But I'm pretty happy anyway. Wonder if you have gone to Norfolk? Hope you have good time.

Fare thee well,

DAD

(Soon after July 4, 1933)

DEAR VERNON,

I thank you for the *State*, and also for having the books sent from the library. I like *State*. Wish I could take it. And the books gave me a very clear idea of the Dewey system, though I would have to have a set of his tables to put the system into effect here.

This has been a cold week here. A fire would have felt good some of the time. The Fourth was very cool. It passed off quietly with me. We seined the pond in the morning and had a ball game in the afternoon. Your Aunt Rena spent the 3rd and 4th with us. Sure glad to see her. She says Roy won a $5 prize at Mars Hill for being best in English. Hal is clerking in store at Jonesboro.

I received a letter today from Robert, Aunt Todie's son, saying that Tody was married June 10 to Mrs. Wayland Rosser. I don't know him.

Mama is going to a cooking demonstration at Jackson Park tonight. Guess I will go on to Concord for an hour or two as I can't cook.

Mrs. Cleaver, better known as Honey, had her tonsils (upper ones I suppose) removed today. Jimmie is a raving maniac in her absence (and worse in her presence).

Andrews has his radio going full blast just across the hall, and my boys are more interested in the ball game being broadcast than in the Settlement of Georgia, so I know poor recitations will result. But I must carry on; so, so long.

DAD

August 8, 1933

DEAR VERNON,

I was afraid you were sick as we did not hear from you last week. I do hope you are well by now, though the flu is so weakening I am afraid you will not feel strong again for some time. Please take good care of yourself and don't take a relapse. A second case is usually worse than a first.

Hope you will get to take your trip to Chicago yet. A good many from this section have gone.

No, the N.R.A.[1] has made no change with our regime at the school. Mr. Morris has an eagle on his windshield, but its a lie or a joke, as he continues, as do we all, to work on thirteen hours.

Mama has been sick for several days. I got her some medicine from Dr. Howard last night and hope it will do her good. I have been waiting on her since I came home, and expect to sit up until she goes to sleep in case I'm needed. So, while I am sitting here on my bed, I am writing this. If you can't read it lay it to the fact that I am using my lap as a desk.

Elroy is working every day—including Sunday. He had to work both Saturday and Sunday. I am very glad for him to have a job, though it won't last very long. He is helping install machinery at the Bleacher.

Another murder in Kannapolis last Saturday. Three murder cases to be tried in Concord this month.

I went to see Brawley about my right eye Sat. Threatened with glaucoma again. Better since treatment. Paper gone.

DAD

August 23, 1933

DEAR VERNON,

So that you may get this before you go to Chicago, I will just write you our little grumble page tonight. First let me say that we

---

[1]National Recovery Act.

are all better, though Mama is still not strong. I got her some medicine that Dr. Howard prescribed Sunday and it has helped her a lot. Think she will be O.K. now.

Bicycling is fine exercise and I am glad you have taken it up. Do you have a wheel?

Should you attempt to go to Chicago on the wheel, you had better start Friday and have a day longer. Anyway, I know you will enjoy the trip. I would like to go, too.

Harold leaves next week.[1] I had planned to take him as I thought I would enjoy the trip, and make it cheaper than he can go on bus, but they don't want me to go, so they changed my mind for me. I guess it is best. Anyway I ought not to lose the time. I've never been so busy as I have been lately. (Gee, what grammar!) Unless something happens soon I think I'll go plum stale. (Gee, what grammar.) It's library, schoolroom, cottage, books, lessons, 028.4, D5, Alger, Boy Scouts, Rover Boys, *Charlotte Observer*, Etta Conley, and an egg for breakfast every day. (Gee, what a world.)

With love,
DAD

October 2, 1933

DEAR VERNON,

It is not because I like this red ink (though I do like it) that I am writing you in the lurid style, but because it is all I have. So, your pardon, please.

We were glad to know that you got back without mishap. I was a little uneasy, of course, but it was because I know so little about that contraption you were riding. I, too, think that country by Asheville, etc. is pretty. I presume you did not stop at Dunlap's.

Nothing new has happened here except that Barber started to the hospital with a boy day before yesterday and stopped to see his sister in Charlotte and the boy jumped out and escaped. Then yesterday he was delivered a boy in Concord who had run away. When he got him back to the school he (the boy) lit from the car first and escaped again. We rag Barber a lot.

---

[1] To enter Appalachian State Teachers' College, Boone, North Carolina.

Mama and I may go to the Baptist State Convention Nov. 15. Not sure yet. I enjoy attending such things as I meet so many old acquaintances.

My ankle is about as it was. Doesn't hurt very much, but aches all the time in a dull kind of way.

Haven't heard from Harold in nearly three weeks. Don't know why he doesn't write. I wrote him again yesterday.

We promoted today, so I have a room full of new boys. I hope they all have lots of ability and are not "slothful in business." But there is poor prospect for that.

I must get busy myself.

With love,
DAD

(Oct., 1933)

DEAR VERNON,

This is letter-writing day, and I am very busy, but while I am waiting for the letters to correct I will write you a few lines as I believe Mama has not written this week. She went to club meeting yesterday and was served ice cream, and to her S.S. class meeting last night and was again served ice cream. Tonight we go to town again and take Roger to Boy Scout meeting and Saturday we, Mrs. Conley, and Lucy Mae Lee go to Charlotte. We plan to take a fried chicken and sandwiches and have a picnic supper.

Elroy went home with Miss Greenlee nearly two weeks ago. Has not come back yet. Roger is picking cotton every day.

I like my new cottage mate very well, though he came, as all new men come, with radical ideas of reform which he is learning won't work. For instance he started out on the principle that kindness was the cure, nay more, the preventive, of all our troubles, and that if the boys were all placed on their honor they would all do right. Fine isn't it? Love rules the world, anyway! But, since one boy gouged out another boy's eye with a stake, and another boy, rejoicing in his newfound freedom, ran away, and still others were having a high revel of debauchery in the bedroom, he is beginning to cut his wisdom teeth.

Hastily,
DAD

(Oct. 9, 1933)

DEAR VERNON,

I have just got a statement from Cline and Moose and it is more than I expected. I am not sure, but I think you paid them $2.60 for me when you were at home. But I was not given credit for it. Do you remember paying them anything for me? Please write me at once stating any facts that might cause them to remember the circumstance. It seems to me that you gave me their receipt, but I have lost it.

All well except my ankle. May move to 12th Cottage this week. Fair next week. Charlotte last Saturday until 10:00 P.M. Elroy back now from Greenlee's. Roger picking cotton. He's a Boy Scout. Mama quilting.

With love,
DAD

Oct. 16, 1933

DEAR VERNON,

This is Fair Week here, and we have been on the "go" so much we have neglected writing to you and Harold. However, Harold turned up last night. He will be here until Monday. I think he is getting along fairly well and is getting some of his ego "busted."

The J.T.S. boys went to the Fair Thursday. I stayed at the school and did police duty but went yesterday. Had passes to all the shows, but went in only three. Mama and boys expect to go to the automobile races this P.M. I can't go.

We have two new men at work here. Ed Poole quit and is on police force at Concord.

DAD

Nov. 17, 1933

DEAR VERNON,

Mama, Mrs. Conley, and I went to the Bapist State Convention at Greensboro Wednesday. We enjoyed the trip very much, even though it was cold and windy. We saw several of our "folks," including Uncle Ike and Aunt Bert, Cousin I. T. Newton from Whiteville, Cousin Will Brooks from Jonesboro, "Rev. Cousin" C. V. Brooks and his son, Rev. Boyce Brooks, from Wacamaw, and several others. Boyce has just entered the ministry and was presented to the convention by his father. We took a fried chicken and ate it for dinner in Greensboro. Stopped at Thomasville that night for supper.

I received a letter yesterday from Elsie Thomas. She is in school at Campbell and getting along nicely. Mildred, her sister, is in Nashville, Tenn., in school of music, and Velma is teaching in Jacksonville. They are fine girls.

Harold spent Sunday at home. He seems to be doing fairly well—not flunking but not making the best of grades. However, he is doing pretty well.

Roger is, as usual, getting along fine in school. And he is a fine boy, too.

Somebody in Raleigh gave my cottage a big Majestic radio. But it won't say a word. Possibly a tube is shot. Hope they will have it fixed before Sunday.

You can tell from this writing that I am rushing it through. So, as it is getting so I can hardly read it myself, I had better stop.

With love,
DAD

Dec. 8, '33

DEAR VERNON,

Glad you got home all right. I was rather uneasy about you since it was so rainy that afternoon. And I was afraid you would catch cold. Somehow I have been "scanlus" well this winter so far. Not even a cold. (I use Mr. Johnson's descriptive adjective.) However I am thankful to be so well. Mama is O.K. too.

I had another letter from Thelma today. She said that after

leaving home she worked for her board and clothes until she got a job. Said she has been in Winston most of the time working in hosiery mill. Was married June a year ago. She and her husband both at work. She says he is a good man—doesn't drink or curse or stay out at night and is so good to her. She said they were very happy. No children. I am glad she seems to be doing so well. She said they were going to drive down to see her mother soon if she would let her come. I wrote to Todie today.

Mama and I expect to go to Charlotte tomorrow. No news other than above.

With love,

DAD

March 4, 1934

DEAR VERNON,

As I wrote you Saturday, Mr. Barber said that Mr. Boger told him not to order shoes for anybody again, as it was against orders of the state purchasing agent. So, I am returning the money. I am sorry we can't order, as I, too, wanted to get a pair for Harold.

Glad that you had so nice a time Easter. It passed off very quietly here. Except for the special services at the church, which were impressive, the day for me was about as any other Sunday. I wanted to go to Winston, but Mama didn't.

Well Elroy is now a businessman. He bought out Whit Pharr's Service Station. He seems to be making some. Of course it won't be much, but I think he can do pretty well at it. The C.W.A.[1] work was a great thing for him.

Haven't heard from Harold in a week or more.

I'm right busy this A.M., so, so long.

DAD

Will you go with Playmakers to Saint Luis?

(March, 1934)

DEAR VERNON,

If Thursday is a pretty day, I will go after books. If it isn't then the next pretty day thereafter. Many thanks to you and Mrs.

---

[1]Civil Works Administration.

Klutts. Mr. Boger will officially write letters of thanks to you and her.

Mama will probably go with me as far as Sanford. I will have to make the round trip in one day.

Will see you in a day or two.

DAD

April 15, 1934
Sunday A.M.

DEAR VERNON,

Just a card to let you know that we are O.K. We each thought the other had written, so neither had.

No news except that Elroy has quit the store. Didn't much more than break even. Eight or ten different ones have tried that place and none have made a living at it.

Love,
DAD

May 2, 1934

Am on my vacation. Am in Troy, on way to Sanford. Will try to see you before I go back. Will be at Cameron tonight.

DAD

May 11, 1934

DEAR VERNON,

It was disappointing to me that we failed to make connections Sunday. I think I met you beyond Bynum. As I was not sure that it was you I went on. No one at your house could tell me about you, so at one o'clock I went to Durham and spent a few hours. Returning by your place, I knocked at the door loud and long but could get no response, so I went back to Bonlee.

We had a very pleasant vacation. Mama was not very well, and got tired out from so much riding. However, she feels better now. We went to Charlotte yesterday.

I came back to work today, and started in with bad luck. I brought quite a lot of stuff with me as I came this A.M., including my Sunday suit. There were some matches in the pocket, and somehow I must have rubbed them with the suitcase. Anyway, they ignited and burnt the whole side of my best coat. It is ruined. I don't know what I am to do, as I have no money to buy another. I may be able to borrow enough to buy a suit, but as Tom Grier is not here, I don't know who has it.

Harold is home. He has improved a good deal, I think.

With love,
DAD

May 17, 1934

DEAR VERNON,

I thank you so much for the loan of the $20. After looking all over Concord, I could not find a suit to fit, so I had Efirds to order me one. Hope it gets here pretty soon, for if anything should happen that I should have to go anywhere, I don't have a suit fit to wear.

Did I tell you that Harold's typewriter was stolen a few days before he came home? He informed the police, but has had no word from them. I guess it is gone for good. Misfortunes never come singly. To add to my woes, Dr. Cadmon said over the radio Sunday that a sure test of one's poetic appreciation was Milton's sonnets, and I don't especially like Milton's sonnets!

Elroy is painting our house. Mama is using the money she made sewing for C.W.A. to buy paint. It looks so much better where he has painted. We will only use one coat (of paint).

Mr. Hudson has left the school, and Mr. and Mrs. Wood will have that cottage, I think. Mr. Cope is now my fellow bond-servant at #12. I like him O.K.

I am glad you had so good a time Sunday. I don't know who the Mrs. Harris is, or was when we knew each other.

Our meeting begins Sunday. Big Jim Somebody or other is to do the preaching. I hope to attend some—if I get my suit.

Mama and all are very well.

With love,
DAD

May 31, 1934

Dear Vernon,

The sun is shining this morning, and I am very glad, as it has been so cold and rainy for a long time. We have not had any coal to burn, but have been burning what trash—roots and stumps—we could find, and that supply has become almost exhausted. But maybe it will be warmer now. I don't want to buy anymore coal.

We are having a splendid meeting at our church. Dr. Kramer, better known as "Big Jim" of Denver, is conducting it. His singer, Grant Sinclare, of Oklahoma, is a golden-voiced tenor that I like very much. I feel that the meeting is one of the best I have ever attended, and I am sure the entire community is receiving a great blessing.

Have you fully decided to sever your connection with News Bureau? I was talking with Lee White again yesterday, and he said that if you would like the experience he thought you might get work with one of our congressmen or senators in Washington. He said he would go with you to see Luther Hartsell who would be glad to use his influence to help you. So, if you would like to try for such a position, I would get Maddry and others to give me letters of recommendation, mentioning your ability with the typewriter, educational qualifications, etc. And then when you come home, you could take the matter up with Mr. Hartsell.

Seems like such a long time since I have seen you. I hope you can be at home soon.

With love,
Dad

June 14, 1934

Dear Vernon,

Dad

P.S. Will write more next time.

104

DEAR VERNON,

It's hot! Just as I came into my schoolroom I noticed the thermometer. It registers 90°. With the heat like that we can't get much done in school, so I, for one, am not trying to do a great deal.

Did you get the things we sent in good shape? Hope we did not overlook anything you wrote for. Have you got any work yet? Was your story accepted by *Mercury*? I think you were indeed fortunate in getting your board and room at so little cost.

Harold and Roger have started back to school. They are both enthusiastic about their work, I am glad to say. Elroy got back day before yesterday from a bumming trip to Washington. He went by freight. Spent two days in Washington. Mrs. Conley spent a week at home. Miss Eva was our matron. Etta is back and Eva will leave soon.

Last night Mama went to a missionary society meeting. I went to town, Elroy went to the store, Harold went swimming, Roger went to Howard's, and the mercury went up. Last night, also, Roy Ritchie caught two thieves trying to steal gas from school's truck, Cleaver caught a boy trying to swallow a chew of tobacco, one of the gas thieves (Buz Corzine) caught Hail Columbia, and I caught a nap about 12 o'clock.

Wish I had about two acres of White Lake to play in. Wish I had a million dollars. If you need anything let me know.

> With love,
> DAD

August 7, 1934

DEAR VERNON,

Your letter was received yesterday, and greatly enjoyed. As to news, it was a failure, but its literary merit is superb. Never have I seen such style, elegant but terse, in any letter—no waste of words, no unnecessary amplifications, no redundance, no hyperbole—just minimum essentials which allow a free use of the imaginative faculties for a correct interpretation of the ideas you so cleverly conveyed; furthermore, it was a deserved reprimand to my dilatoriness in writing to you, but, inasmuch as I had written to you only two days prior to the receipt of your letter (though in all probability you had not received it at the time your communication was made to me), I think that at this particular time when the self-expressionists are earnestly advocating the discontinuance of all forms of punishment, so that one may follow the natural trend of one's own inclinations, being firm in their belief that when one is so permitted, unhampered by supervision, unrestrained by the fear of punishment, his natural abilities, his innate goodness will predominate—I say that at this particular time, your letter is untimely in that it bears the earmark of punishment, and as such, it, methinks, would be condemned by any society, whether local or national, which has for its objective the correction of fault, the rehabilitation of those whom unmerciful disaster has almost crushed, and this without any kind of punishment whatsoever.

Mama had a very enjoyable trip. She is well.

I am well, but not having an enjoyable trip anywhere, except my trip home every night.

The rest are so so, except Roger, who is just O.K.

Lardner Query is working here.

I went to see Dr. Brawley Sunday.

Mama is canning peaches.

Mrs. Walker has gone to hospital in Atlanta.

Little boys under 11 years have been segregated. One of them asked Dr. Buie if segregation and castration were the same. He assured them that it was painless. Scarboro will have little boys' cottage.

DAD

Aug. 23, 1934

DEAR VERNON,

I thank you for doing the typing. I may send the thing to Goerch for his rejection, but I am not sure—it's such a silly mess, but with a grain of truth in it.

The enclosed clipping from *Observer* has created quite a good deal of comment locally.

I hope your application with Thrift Society goes through O.K. Do you like the work? Will you be with Symphony Orchestra again later? Has Trouble returned?

I may send Harold to Brevard College this year. Cheaper there. Would credits from Brevard be accepted at Chapel Hill? He can get some work at Brevard.

I'm pretty busy today, can't write much.

Love,
DAD

August 28, 1934

DEAR VERNON,

Your pictures, especially the one with side view, are very good. We appreciate them. Where were they taken? Hope your work will be pleasant and profitable with Thrift Society. (My! What English.) Just what is that society? I am unacquainted with it.

Mama has been sick abed since Friday. She seems better this afternoon, and I hope she will soon be up.

Thelma, her husband, her two brothers, Wilbur and Robert, were at our house Sunday. Fortunately, Mrs. Conley had cooked a chicken for us, so they had something to eat.

I sent Goerch[1] my piece. Haven't had it returned yet. The enclosure I failed to make in my last letter will be in this. I have received favorable comment from several places—Charlotte, Mooresville, Concord.

With love,
DAD

Sept. 1, 1934

DEAR VERNON,

Mama is somewhat better. Sat up most of the afternoon yesterday, after having been in bed a week. If she is able, I'll bring her to the school for dinner today.

According to *The State*, I am a fellow by the name of Croom. He believes some things I don't; but any way a few dollars extra

---

[1]Carl Goerch, editor of *The State* magazine.

come in mighty handy. I may try some more stunts in writing—
for the love of it, and for the money. Goerch gave me front page.

DAD

Sept. 6, 1934

DEAR VERNON,

Strike—strike—strike! Tha's all I hear at this place—that and
the peculiar circumstances surrounding the death of Miss Jenn
Cothrane.

Mama is some better. She is up some of the time now. She was
in bed ten or twelve days. Took her to see the doctor again
Monday, and he seems to have done her a lot of good.

Harold is going to Brevard College this year. Cheaper than
Boone. He leaves the 15th. I may take him. 'Twould be a nice
outing. Harold is not very well. Sore throat and sore feet. J.T.S.
boys run off every day. Very unruly. I'm regusted.

Will be so glad if you can get home for a visit. Seems like I
haven't seen you in a long time. You must have kept the keys hot
to have written so much.

Love,
DAD

Oct. 28, 1934

Glad you received Lineberry's letter. I was afraid it had been lost.
Mama and I just got back from a visit to Jo Cox's, about 10 miles
from Concord. Most attractive home and charming family of two
brothers and one sister, all past 50 years of age. Mama seems
some better. I have bronchitis. Elroy has another Ford—a coupe.

DAD

Nov. 7, '34

DEAR VERNON,

Glad to get your letter yesterday. Hadn't heard from you in a
long time. Wish I could be there with you. Weather nice and cool
here. Mama still taking treatment, but is much better. Think she
will soon be O.K. Elroy got laid off last week. No work now.
There is a letter here for you from *American Magazine.* Looks

like a returned manuscript. I got a similar one from *Colliers.* Harold on student council at Brevard. Latchstring is hanging out for you.

Dad

(Nov. or Dec., 1934)

Dear Vernon,

Yesterday my three minutes talk with you passed so fast that I did not get to ask you if you got your money order. I mailed it to you Saturday in care of Margaret. I hope you got it O.K.

You sounded hoarse over the phone. I hope you do not have cold. It was nice to hear your voice again, even if it was hoarse.

Am anxious to know how you came out with the Alexander proposition. I hope it was something you want, and will like.

If your licenses come, what shall I do with them?

We are all well. I am back in school. Had another piece in last week's *State.* Sent him another yesterday—"My Christmas Cow."

Please write as soon as you can, and tell me all about your job, if any. And if you have no work, we want you to come home and stay where it won't cost you a cent if you can stand our faces.

There is a chance that Elroy will go to C.C.C.[1] Will know tomorrow. It will be a great help if he gets in. Harold may go back to Brevard tomorrow. He thinks he can get some work in library 'till school opens. Roger starts to school today.

With love,
Dad

Jan. 5, 1935

Dear Vernon,

We are sending suitcase this afternoon. Hope we get everything in it that you want. If not will send it later.

What kind of work do you do? I hope it is something you like.

No sign of your license yet. You had better investigate.

Harold left for Brevard Thursday. Elroy failed to get in C.C.C. Roger is in school again.

---

[1]Civilian Conservation Corps.

109

Goerch returned my "Cow" piece. Said he had received one from you just before. He said the cow must have been a big event with us. I have no other piece in view. He published one last week.

Did you enjoy your trip to Raleigh? How is Gertrude? And the rest?

We are all well.

Write me the news.

Love,
DAD

(Feb., 1935)

DEAR VERNON,

It is very cold this morning—has been cold for a week, despite the fact that JoJo has been saying fair and warmer. It snowed a few minutes here Sunday, but not much. I hope it will turn warmer before Saturday as Mama says I may go to Charlotte then, and I am looking forward to it as a break in the "Montoniousness" (as Mr. Walker says) of this place. It's getting on my nerves. One boy ran off last week, broke in a store in Salisbury, stole three pistols, and threatened to shoot the cop who got him. He was a new boy. Another new boy ran off and stole $350 and a motorcycle in Charlotte, went to Raleigh, put up as a hotel detective, and held up the welfare officer who tried to arrest him. The cops got him later. Still another ran off, stole a Chevrolet in Concord and wrecked it at Harrisburg going 55 miles an hour. He was unhurt, more's the pity. We have more of that kind of gang material than ever before. And we are expected to coddle them, feed them on sweet talk, and let them defy us. I would as soon go to jail as to the insane asylum.

Do you like your new job?

Time for class. So long.

DAD

P.S. Elroy is a P.W.A.[1] timekeeper. 20¢ an hour.

---

[1]Public Works Administration.

March 14 (1935)

DEAR VERNON,

It has been such a long time since I have written a letter that I am out of practice, but maybe this will contain something that will interest you anyway. But what it is to be, is a mystery to me, as all I know is what I see by the papers—and I don't have the chance often of seeing a paper. However, the spirit of unrest which according to Grady Cole is pervading the criminal world and the prison life of North Carolina as a result of recent happenings in Charlotte, has hit this place kerslam! The boys, the unspanked product of flannel-hearted public opinion, are running off daily and getting by with a polite "please be good, and you may go home soon." When they curse the officers and tell them they won't do a d— thing, and call the matron a liar, it ought to please Mrs. Kate Burr and her coterie of molycoddlers (I don't know how to spell it) to hear us say in gentle tones: "Now Son, it isn't pretty to talk like that! Here, eat this ice cream and tonight I'll take you to see a wild West show, if you will be a sweet little boy," or some such rot as that. By golly, wish I had $40,000,000! I'd retire.

My eye continues to bother me. Am taking treatment from Dr. McCutcheon, of Salisbury. I don't use my eyes any more than I have to—so Carl Goerch must let his paper suffer. Anyway, I'm mad with him as I got a rejection slip from him a month ago for the best piece I ever wrote—"The Phoenix Man"—inspired by one of your verses. Goerch said it was splendid essay, but not for the *State*.

Every time I start to write these angel boys start raising cain, so goodbye.

DAD

March 5, 1935

DEAR VERNON,

Last night some sixty or more cows went A.W.O.L. (absent with out leave) from the Training School pasture. Mr. Kiser and some of the boys tried to head them off and turn them back, but they stampeded. To the railroad they ran in a compact mass of wild milk cows, and then down the tracks as far as the Lady place. The boys could not turn the leaders of those cows who led their followers right on into the jaws of death. A fast, north-bound passenger train, making sixty miles an hour, rounded the curve just ahead of the cut into which the cows had rushed. There was a grinding of brakes. The whistle screamed in affright, but for thirteen of those fine milk cows nemeses was at hand. The train hit them with a sickening thud. The nose of the cowcatcher was rammed in the ground and the train almost derailed. Thirteen dead cows!

The engineer alighted and yelled: "Where in the h— am I—in Texas? I never saw so many cows anywhere else!" That's that.

May I advise that when you throw shoes across creeks hereafter that you get a pocket full of silver dollars and first practice throwing them across the Potomac—or maybe I mean the James—like your distinguished countryman of former years— the late George Washington, esq.

My motto, or slogan, is: "Happy on the way." I am trying to live up to it, even if I'm broke as a convict. Month before last I found myself at the end of month with no cash and some debts. Last month less cash and more debts. This month on the 5th, more and bigger and finer debts. So, I'm still happy on the way.

Elroy was laid off for two or three weeks, but is again back on the job. Don't know how long it will last. Harold will be home Easter.

Love,
DAD

(April, 1933)

DEAR VERNON,

If you find any meaning in that that I am about to write, please inform me, for really to designate what I am about to write—for if the sheet fits into a letter it will be a miracle. I ain't got no idea in my head but books—books, ragged, dirty books. This deplorable condition is caused by the fact that I have been working every moment of the day at recess and after school in the library recataloging them according to a system I've developed to facilitate the distribution of the books.

David Copperfield is being presented in Concord. I would like to have seen it but—

Maybe the Townsend Bill will put me on easy street some day.

Mama will not get to go to Sanford Easter as Mrs. Lang has appendicitis and not able to travel.

Roger is looking forward to his trip to Chapel Hill with lots of enthusiasm. Wish I could work up some enthusiasm for sumpen!

Harold spends Easter at home. We will be glad to see him. Wish you could be home too.

I can't squeeze another idea out of my mind, so *bon nuit*.

DAD

I love you.

April 23, 1935

DEAR VERNON,

Anent the man of mystery you met on the stair, I have had an experience quite as peculiar:

> My pay this April acted quare,
> I got a raise that wasn't there;
> It won't be there again in May—
> I wonder why it's gone away!

Luke, no its Mark 6:3: "Is not this the carpenter, the son of Mary, the brother of James, and Joses, and of Juda, and Simon? And are not his sisters here with us?" Question: How many sisters? And who?

There is nothing I had rather do then to attend that week of merrymaking at Chapel Hill, and be a Boy Scout, a dogwood, a playmaker, or a rock garden. I think the last mentioned would be most desirable. Oh, to be just a rock garden with nothing to do but just to sit still and be surrounded by beautiful flowers, cool pools, and lovely college girls! (Mustn't let Mama see this!)

We did not mean for you to pay Roger's expenses at all. I shall pay you back some day. Seems like I just get further and further in debt to you. But now that Elroy has gone to C. C. Camp, he will give me ten dollars a month, and I hope soon to be able to pay all my obligations. Though my head is bloody, it is still unbowed, and when I get my debts paid, I'll even wash off the blood and jeer at the Depression that has tried to beat me up.

Roger certainly is a fine boy. We are proud of him. He is so happy in his anticipation of a good time at Chapel Hill.

Harold's report was better last quarter. I hope he can get work this summer and save enough so that within a year he can finish his college course. I cannot pay all of his expenses another year.

I shall ask—nay, I shall order—Mama to add something hereunto that may be of interest to you. I have run out except to say I didn't see your piece in paper as I don't take one. I shall look for your story in *Observer* if I can find one. Now Mama's time.

DAD

(May or June, 1935)

DEAR VERNON,

Our little trip to Brevard was very pleasant and was enjoyed even by Mama who hitherto has been easily tired on a journey the length of that. But due to the comfort of the new Chevy, she got along fine. We spent the night at Judge English's in Brevard and it was so cold that they had a fire. We ran into a rain at Lake Lure on our way up. Sunday morning we drove out to Conestee Falls, about 10 miles from Brevard. I was more impressed with these falls than with the Linville Falls, though the volume of water may not be as great. One of Harold's friends, Leggett, of Halifax County, came home with us and spent the night, after which he had to Leggitt home (pardon).

We were so glad to have you at home a few days. I was in the clover field when you left, though that doesn't mean that I was exactly "in clover" with the sun blistering my skin. Yesterday Mr. Johnson, Mr. Andrews, Mr. Boysworth, and I took about 150 boys to Kress's Lake for a swim and hot dog roast. Compliments of Lions' Club. Big time.

These ?1x-: Ox boys are keeping so much racket when I get busy writing that I'll just stop and tend to 'em.

DAD

114

July 19, 1935

DEAR VERNON,

I don't know whether Mama has written to you this week or not, so I will write a line or two.

Roger is much better. He is not very strong yet, but has a growing appetitie, so I guess he will be all right. Dr. Ketner first pronounced it appendicitis, but after keeping an ice cap on his "belly" (as Ketner said) for 24 hours, the case didn't develop, so he treated him for biliousness with fine results. (Supply the other L; it is needed to spell the disease referred to.)

I took Mrs. Conley to the depot this A.M. She is on her way to California. She takes Elizabeth and—what's her name?—the next oldest girl of Sam's with her.

Harold has no work yet. He has gone to Charlotte to see about a job advertised in *Observer*.

Conley took us to see *Jean Val Jean* this week. It's a fine picture. Well-played.

The Campbells are coming, so I'll attack them with some words to spell.

Love,

DAD

9/10/35

DEAR VERNON,

We have not heard from you since your operation. We are uneasy. Please get someone to write us a card—if you are not able to write—and let us know how you are.

Love,

DAD & CO.

Monday A.M.

DEAR VERNON,

I certainly wish I could do what you suggest in your letter, but until something cracks I can't. I have been out 4½ days already and can't lose any more time if I can help it. I am at work now but am still "kinder" shabby. Am taking some of Dr. Yow's nerve medicine and two other kinds for bronchitis. Guess I will be O.K.

115

soon. Harold says he will pay for the time I lost.

Son, I hope I can pay you some on what I owe you this month. Elroy says I can have $12 out his check this time. I know you need the money, as you were in hospital so long.

Roger is president of his class at Concord High. We are proud of him.

I hope to be relieved of cottage duty for awhile.

Love,

DAD

Oct. 1, 1935

DEAR VERNON,

I am feeling better this A.M. Had a good night's sleep last night—first one in a week or more.

Hope you are getting over your operation O.K. Sure must take care not to ride too soon.

DAD

Oct. 9, 1935

DEAR VERNON,

Folks have been mighty nice to me. While I was sick a big basket of flowers came from Mrs. Sappenfield; a fine box of homemade walnut and cherry candy from Lucy May Lee; a two pound box of homemade mints from Myrtle Thomas; delicious chocolate fudge from Mama; a bill saying I owed Dr. Yow $3.00; a dun from Porter Drug Co., for $11.45 for vile tasting medicine of four different brands of nastiness; a bill from A. B. Pounds for $7.98 for a ton of black, sooty coal; a nice yellobole pipe from Harold; word that Roger was made president of his class in Concord; a dun for the $10.00 I owed Haden Talbert, and many other delightful experiences.

Then came Roger's birthday and my own. We celebrated together Sunday. Mama and Roger gave me a hat; Greenlee and Conley gave me a tie, and Roger a tie; Myrtle and Lucy May gave us a splendiferous birthday cake—angel food cake, with 15 candles on it. (Why they made angel cake instead of devil's food cake I dunno.) Harold gave me a subscription to *Concord*

Tribune, and somebody—Conley, I strongly suspect—sent me an all-day sucker, nicely done up in a big box. Wonder what she thinks I am—a baby? Mama had a fine dinner of chicken. There were three dead ones on the table and Greenlee, Lucy May, Conley, and Myrtle sitting at the table. I love chickens, old hens, and all. John Bolton of Concord and John Volmer of Kannapolis were also present. We had a good time. To be fifty years old ain't so bad.

Mrs. Presson died of pneumonia at the school Sunday night.

Mr. Lee, brother of Mrs. Lee, matron at #2, is in Charlotte Hospital with pneumonia. He is very low, if still alive.

Feels good to be off cottage duty for awhile, even if my wages should be cut.

Wish I could see you. I hope you take good care not to do anything that would bring on a recurrence of your former trouble.

I have been on lookout for a car, but haven't found one yet.

Love,

DAD

Nov. 7, 1935

DEAR VERNON,

I didn't sleep much last night and so I feel drowsy today. At 12 last night I got up and went in front room to sit awhile in the hopes of getting sleepy, but all I got was cold.

I ordered me a suit yesterday. Elroy gave Mama and me $25, so we are both getting a suit. She is going to get hers this afternoon, but I had to have mine made.

We went to see Will Rogers in *Doubting Thomas* last Monday night. Mrs. Conley's treat. Not so good as other plays of his to my notion.

How do you like Velma? She is just O.K. I think.

Hope you can come to see us soon.

DAD

Feb. 5, 1936

DEAR VERNON,

What I dislike most, in so far as the weather is concerned is a long, continued cold spell, with lots of snow and rain and slush underfoot, and in the head and chest, too. In short, a bad cold in weather and body. I hope it will soon be warm and sunny again. Coal bills and medicine bills have been very high this winter.

Chapel Hill is getting a lot of publicity. I regret the notoriety that has been given the boys, and wish the names of the students, guilty though they were, could have been kept from the papers. It is hard on them and on their parents. But it is fine of the student council to clean the unsavory mess up. Do you know whether Hubert Rand is the grandson of Capt. Rand, former steward at State School for the Blind? If so, he is a first cousin of Soliciter Warren Williams of Sanford.

I have not heard from Grissett about insurance. Maybe his scheme is for the university folks only.

I have not sent for the belt material yet, as my dollars have been too scarce. I shall try to order it next month, however.

We will take your typewriter to Lemon Springs when we go. But we will not make that trip until the weather gets warmer.

Mirabile dictu, one boy of mine has been exempted from a math exam! His name is Roger.

Class time.

With love,

DAD

Feb. 26, 1936

If nothing happens we will see you at Rob's Sunday. Will take typewriter and radio. Hope Mildred will come too. Wish Velma could be there. Would it be much out of the way to come by Bonlee?

Hope flu is well.

DAD

Wed. A.M.

(March 18, 1936)

DEAR VERNON,

Glad you are coming home. Bring Mildred. It may be dull for her since Harold will be in hospital. He goes to Charlotte to Eye,

Ear, & Throat Hospital today for operation. We are very uneasy about him. Mama will be with him, and I will go over this P.M.

See you tomorrow.

DAD

March 20, 1936

DEAR VERNON,

We are sorry that you could not get to come home. Hope you can come soon anyway.

Harold had a rather serious operation. The tumor was larger than a big hen egg. Dr. Motley says it was the most serious operation he had performed in 15 years. Mama stays with him during day. We have special nurses for him night and day, but I think we can dismiss them today. Dr. says we can. I go over to see him every day after school.

I can't write very well but maybe you can read it. I'm O.K. but nervous.

With love,
DAD

(Late March—early
April 1936)

DEAR SON,

I am glad to say that Harold is recovering very rapidly. He goes back to the hospital for examination today. Dr. Peeler says it was not cancer, for which we are thankful. Harold hopes to go back to work next week. I told him to ask the doctor's advice about it.

I suppose every unperverted son of Adam feels the call of spring to get out of the four walls within which he has been pent for the long winter months, and back in the sunshine of these glorious days. Anyway, I wish I could have a few days free from the madding crowd of Jackson Training School boys—and officers. But I will not have much vacation this year, as most of the 15 days that have been allowed us for vacation has already been used up with sickness.

Yesterday I received a card from the water concern saying "No charge for the quarter." How come, I wonder? Anyway, it saved me about $3.00. I have wanted to pay you what I owe you for a long time, so I will use the unexpected $3.00 to make a little payment on my debt. I will try to get it all paid within a few months. And, by the way, we are expecting a new calf within a month or two. The cow has certainly been a boon to us. The calf should bring you a few dollars more.

We got a shipment of books for our library from Raleigh last week, and on the fly leaf of many of them I noticed such familiar names as: Hardy Murphree Ray, John E. Ray, Mrs. Brinson, and Frank Simpson. Those names brought up pleasant memories of the past.

As ever,

DAD

I seem to be stuck "within." I notice that word four or five times in this letter. But it's a good word.

April 23, 1936

DEAR VERNON,

I was not very well last night, and this morning I stayed at home, but am at work this afternoon. I have dysentery—or sumthen. Paregoric seems to have been effective. Anyway, I feel better.

Mama has gone to a club meeting over near Poplar Tent, Harold is at work, and Roger is in school; so, what would have been the use of staying at home this P.M. when there would have been no one to hear me grunt?

It seems that your advertising did pay. Hope you continue to get all the typing you want to do. I notice there are to be government exams for typists soon. Salary $1,400.

I have just read *Song of Sixpence*, by Kummer. It's interesting. Haven't seen a show in months.

Can't write a legible hand today, as I'm shaky, so will stop.

DAD

May 8, 1936

DEAR VERNON,

Commencement is on at Harrisburg and while Mama is attending it tonight I shall go to Charlotte to see if I can get me a suit. The weather is so hot I want some cooler clothes. It's very dry here, too. Roger has a *Tribune* route and to attend school, work the paper route, keep stove wood, and milk keeps him busy. But he is on honor roll.

DAD

May 29, 1936

DEAR VERNON,

The Bogers—Chas. E., his wife, Elise, Sara, John, and James—have gone to Cuba and Nassau for a ten day vacation. So, since the cat is away, we mice will have a chance to play. I fear, however, that the cheese has been securely locked in the vault—which is mice proof—and guarded by Mr. Jesse Fisher. I hope they (the Bogers and the mice) will enjoy the vacation.

As for this particular *mice*, I won't have much vacation this year, as eleven of my fifteen days have already been taken. Most of it was spent in bed with my nerves beating a wild tattoo on my enfeebled brain. I don't know when I can get the remaining four days, nor what I can do with them unless I get sick again.

Roger has a chance to spend a week at Ridgecrest—expenses paid—sometime this summer. The trip will be given by B.Y.P.U. to the one having highest rate in the Union. He is tied so far with one other boy for that place. If the tie remains unbroken, I hope both may go. But I presume there will be only one to go.

Harold's throat seems O.K. But somehow he is not very strong, but keeps at work. Mama and I are well.

Enough of this uninteresting personal piffle! And since I know of nothing else to write about save politics, which I don't know at all, and which is also becoming uninteresting, I will stop.

WILLIAM M. CROOK

July 6, (1936)

DEAR VERNON,

We are nicely located at Black Mountain, five miles from Ridgecrest. Miss Greenlee is with us, and we expect Mildred today. I have one bad eye tied up. Wish you were with us. Don't know when we will go home.

DAD

(Fall, 1936)

DEAR VERNON,

Mama told me to write you a note and ask you to let us know whether you and Hettie and Mabel will come on Friday or Saturday, so we can kill the fatted hen. Hope you can come this weekend, as I am not on duty. Can't you?

Mama has not been very well for some time, but is better. I am going over to get her bottle filled now.

DAD

August 13, 1936

DEAR VERNON,

Old men clutter up the face of the earth like derelict Model T's along the highway of life. They are just not needed. The older I get—and I am now an old man—the more I realize that old age is an ugly boil on the face of progressing civilization. It's there, but it certainly isn't wanted, and, so far as I know, isn't needed. Even if a boil is worth $5.00, half-eagles would be accepted for the nasty things by the gross, or cord, or mile, or by whatever measure may be applied to boils.

Boils are not needed in political parties. They are liable to get sore, run, and mess up things for the grand old party. Take Mr. Hoey, for instance, McDonald thinks, and so do many others, that he is a carbuncle on the neck of the party. As a boil myself, I'm glad to have a fellow citizen for my governor. He and I, and thousands of pus-filled excrescences, will soon be lanced, and then, with the pus drained out, only the scar on some part of the anatomy of the body politic will be left to bring painful memories.

A boil in the church is not needed either. Old men who can contribute very little to the finances of the church, who cannot attend its services, and who are never called upon for anything, are certainly not necessary. But as a boil on the brow sticks closer than a hatband, so as a church boil, I'll stick closer and closer to it and its teachings until the lancet removes me. But I sometimes wonder if some good folks don't delight in slapping us old boils just to see us squirm—or do they do it thoughtlessly? I am all kinds of a boil, but as a church boil I suffer most from my own uselessness, inability, and touchiness.

In the home an old man is a boil de lux. With the exception of the wife who, bless her heart, believes that her espoused boil is worth at least $5.00, he is not needed by any other member after the children have become self-sustaining.

With these lamentations de senectute, I will say that we are all well and happy. Had a big time at reunion. Brought Elsie with us. She is a fine girl.

DAD

August 26, 1936

DEAR VERNON,

I thank you for the copies of Rev. Mr. Crook's letter which I received last week. I am afraid it was an imposition on you to write so many. Anyway, I thank you.

It is nice for Josephine to get the work you are furnishing her. Doubtless they will find it pretty hard to make a living and it will help them a lot, I know, for her to have some work.

Hope you find the title is clear to the land you have bought, and that you will find in it, and the house you will build on it, the fulfillment of your dreams. Maybe when I get my old age pension I would like to build a home near you.

Mama has not been very well some days. She has her first cold of serveral years, and is suffering with rheumatism. She got her rheumatism prescription refilled and since taking it, she is better.

Dr. Yow, whom I consulted Saturday about my sprained ankle, gave me some hot liniment to rub on it, and said to stay off my feet and have a picture of ankle made. I'll rub on the hot liniment, but I ain't agonna have no picture made of my pet ankle, and I'm agonna use my ankle whenever I can.

Time for English class. (Judge by this letter whether the study of English is needed!)

DAD

October 12, 1936

DEAR VERNON,

Automobilambulators march on! Just as there is a tide in the affairs of men, so there is the human automobilambulator which we enter at birth, and which bears us on to the glory or the horror of life's sunset. My personal auto (short for automobilambulator) has just completed fifty-two years of service. It is an old model, but, unlike man-made machines, the older it gets the faster it goes. Back in the testing teens, the tempestuous twenties, and even in the thriving thirties, the thing crept from year to year. It required much fuel and emitted much gas, but it just kept increasing its speed very slowly. Those were the years when it tried to make a show. It was then bright and shin(e)y in appearance, and felt itself so strong that it would have undertaken to bear the burden of the world in its rumble seat. And why not? Then Dirty Dan Carbon hadn't corroded its spark plugs, nor had its battery deteriorated through constant use. Its generator produced enough current to keep the motor going and to toot its horn. Especially to toot its horn.

During the frenzied forties, its chassis began to creak and rattle, the horn was about tooted out from constant use, the headlights became dim, the paint wore off, and the tires became more and more patched as a result of the numerous punctures they received—mostly from the porcupine quills that I carelessly pulled from my wounded feelings when things went wrong, and strewed in the path of my automobilambulator. But its speed increased at great rate!

Now it dashes on with me well into the fat fifties. After this? Maybe on into the aching eighties, even, the thing may bear me. ???

What a road it has borne me over! It is strait and narrow—strait because it is hard to keep from turning off into some of the alluring, broad roads to the right and left, and narrow because it's just a single-track way with no returning traffic. The millions of machines along this road must ever retain their relative positions like the stars in the universe. If they take to the detours they have to go so much faster to get back to their place in line. Detours are hard on the humano-automobilambulator. The increased speed required to get back in line burns out bearings. But enough of this.

At last I have an easy chair. For my birthday Mama gave me $10 to apply on it, and Perry-Mincy Co. gave credit for the rest— no not the rest, but the balance. The *rest* I take every night when I sink into its comfortable depths.

Miss Thomas is looking for Velma this weekend.

My leg is better, but still swells. Varicose veins.

DAD

Tuesday A.M.
(Nov., 1936)

DEAR VERNON,

We have not heard from you in two weeks, and we are just a little uneasy, as you have always been so good to write every week. The mail has just come and I was disappointed in not getting a letter today. Please write me a card or letter at once, if you can, and 'splain yo'self.

Harold and Webb went to Lemon Springs and Bonlee Sunday in Webb's car. Thought maybe you would be there, too.

All teachers here have been in field for a week, but due to sprained ankle I've not been able to work.

Hope to hear from you.

FATHER

Dec. 15, 1936

DEAR VERNON,

Harold had an attack of acute appendicitis. We took him to Concord hospital. He is on operating table now. Dr. says he will be all right, as he got there before it got very bad. Will write again tomorrow.

DAD

They just called me from hospital. Said the operation was over, and that Harold was resting very well. Said his appendix were in very bad condition.

Dec. 16, 1936

DEAR VERNON,

Harold was getting along very well when we left hospital last night, except for nausea. Mama will go back over there at noon. Harold is badly discouraged.

DAD

Jan. 14, 1937

DEAR VERNON,

Kate Smith has just taken the place of grouchy old Boke Carter. Harold is at a party in Kannapolis at Jazzie Moore's. Roger is at a party in Concord. Mama and I are in our shirt-sleeves attending Kate S's party at my house. Mama has a cold. I'm feeling fine. Myrtle has come back. Lucy Mae Lee is in hospital. Eva says Etta finds fault with all she does. I don't. She has hot biscuits for supper. Donations received this week: 4 pig feet, 6 collards, some turnips, and a shock of tops! No room on card for paragraphing. Kate has got under my skin.

DAD

Feb. 11, 1937

DEAR VERNON,

When Shakespeare said, " 'Tis the eye of childhood that fears a painted Devil," he could not have known how an old maid in the year 1937 would look when she tries to renew her youth like the eagles.

Did Shakespeare have in mind the Supreme Court of the United States when he said: "The sleeping and the dead are but as pictures?" Or did he have reference to the dry forces in the North Carolina Legislature?

If Shakespeare had been compelled to lose three days from his work on account of flu and resultant backache, and that when he was on a short hour week—not on cottage duty—in the month of February, when a day's work brings $3.05, could he have written: "Sweet are the uses of adversity, which, like the toad, ugly and venomous, wears yet a precious jewel in his head"?

If Shakespeare could meet a modern sophomore named

Horatio, could he still say: "There are more things in heaven and earth, Horatio, than are dreamed of in your philosophy"?

If Shakespeare were living in Hollywood (spelled right?) today, would he decide that the question is not "To be or not to be," but "to Reno or not to Reno! That's the question. Whether 'tis nobler of the mind to suffer the jeers and banters of the wives we have, or fly to others we know not of"?

"When shall we three meet again?" That's easy. When my creditors, my debtors, and I quit hounding one another.

Anyway, this letter is just like I feel—crazy, ironical, satirical, uncharitable, uncouth, coarse, vulgar, flippant, unsightly, ridiculous, silly, mean, ugly—and if there be any other adjective that may apply to a fellow with flu, for Pete's sake use it! I've been in bed three days and by now I'm a holy pain in the neck.

Dad

April 24, 1937

Dear Vernon,

I expect to take your mother to Charlotte this afternoon to consult Dr. Brenizer about her condition. She has not been well for six weeks or more, and Dr. Yow in Concord, who has been treating her for more than a month, does not seem to help her any. Dr. Brenizer is supposed to be the best in this section. He certainly charges enough to be good, but I won't mind that if he can do her any good.

Today is cool, quite different from yesterday. It looks like rain.

Mr. Lawrence let his boys throw ball near where my car was parked, and they broke my windshield. Cost $15.08. Lawrence says he will pay for it. Maybe he will. Why did your battery go dead? It is mail time.

Dad

Sunday
(April 25, 1937)

Dear Vernon,

I took Mama to see Dr. Brenizer yesterday and he advises an immediate operation. She plans to enter Sanitarium in Charlotte

Thursday. She has some kind of growth inside. Dr. says it is not a cancer, but may become one if allowed to remain. She also has a cyst on ovary which must be removed.

I pray God to direct the surgeon's hand and save my wife.

YOUR FATHER

(April 26, 1937)
Monday

DEAR VERNON,

Mama has decided to go to hospital Wednesday. Am writing Dr. Brenizer today. I will keep you informed every day.

YOUR FATHER

April 28, '37

VERNON,

Mama was on table 1 hour 20 minutes. Dr. says she stood it fine and is doing all right. I am so thankful.

DAD

April 29, '37
Thursday

Mama continues to improve. Is resting well. Hypo does that. She will have to be here at least two weeks. I am to bring Mrs. Conley over this P.M. for operation. Thyroid.

DAD

April 30, 1937
Friday A.M.

DEAR VERNON,

This is the third day since Mama's operation. She is weak but getting along very well. These good doctors and nurses don't mean to let her suffer. I am thankful she is getting along so well.

DAD

May 1, 1937
Saturday

DEAR VERNON,

Mama got by with her third day very well. She was nervous and suffered some. Dr. says she will be better today. No company allowed yet. I will not go to Charlotte till P.M. today.

DAD

May 3, 1937
Sunday 5 P.M.

VERNON,

Mama had a very good day today. She's getting sassy. Wants to be moved down to Mrs. Conley's room. Will move her tomorrow. Lots of company and flowers.

DAD

May 4, 1937
Tuesday A.M.

DEAR VERNON,

I had Mama moved down to a quieter room yesterday. The one she had was so noisy. It faced the elevator, and so many people congregated at the door jabbering at high speed while waiting for elevator. She is now in room with Mrs. Conley. They both seem to be doing fine. Mama talked more last night than she has done in a week. Elroy came to see her Sunday.

DAD

May 5, 1937

DEAR VERNON,

Yesterday afternoon when I went to Charlotte I found Mama feeling pretty well. She talked more than she has before, and seemed to be in good spirits, and enjoyed a laugh or two, even in the face of the hospital bill I had to pay for her first week there— $52.00. Her hospital bill will not be so much this week. I am afraid her doctor will charge $150, but I don't care if it is a thousand dollars. I will gladly pay on it month by month until it is all paid. I am just so happy to think that she will be benefited. For several years she has been so poorly. Now I believe she will be much better. If she would only eat. They bring such nice meals, but she barely touches them. Drinks a little milk or soup.

Elroy came Sunday. He spends every cent he makes—$30 per month. I asked him if he could give Mama a few dollars each month to help pay her bills, but he made no answer.

Did I tell you what Mama got rid of in her operations? She lost a benignant tumor on uterus, a cyst on ovary, her appendix, and some hemorrhoids.

Mrs. Conley is getting along fine. She has had special nurses day and night, but I think she has not needed them. The regular nurses gave Mama good care.

I hope you can come this weekend.

DAD

May 6 (1937)

VERNON,

I was so glad to find Mama looking and feeling better last night. Mrs. Conley also. Hope she will be home in a week or ten days.

Robert Crook came last night.[1] He is a fine looking boy.

DAD

Friday A.M.
(May 7, 1937)

DEAR VERNON,

Your mother had a rather bad day yesterday, but seemed to be resting better last night. When I go over there this afternoon I hope to find her more comfortable.

DAD

May 12, 1937

DEAR VERNON,

As I have no other kind of paper, I'll use this. Mother is getting along very well. She is to call me today and let me know whether or not she can come home this afternoon. I do hope she can

---

[1]Son of Alex Crook.

come, but I want her to stay in hospital until the doctor says she can come.

Miss Greenlee and Miss Thomas went down home last night and "cleaned up" for her. It was kind of them. Everyone has been so good.

Rev. Mr. Spence is to be buried today. Mrs. Taylor was buried yesterday.

Hastily,
DAD

May 13, 1937

DEAR VERNON,

I brought Mama home safely yesterday afternoon. She made the trip in a new DeLux Chevrotet without much discomfort, and slept well last night. We are fortunate in having a good Negro woman to stay with us. Dr. Brenizer was very reasonable in his charge—$100.00. I gave him a note. Thanks to you, her hospital bill—$98—is paid.

"It never rains but it pours."

"Troubles never come singly but in battalions."

"Under the bludgeonings of chance, my head is bloody but unbowed."

All of which may be summed up, so far as the house of Crook is concerned, by saying: Yesterday morning Harold stayed at home from his work to go to Bost's Mill for the Negro to stay with us, and to help get Mama home in the afternoon. On his way for the Negro he failed to make a sharp left turn in the road. The car turned over one or two times and landed on its wheels in a field. Harold had two tendons cut in left wrist, a bad gash on forearm, and a scalp wound. A passing motorist took him to hospital. He lost a lot of blood and was very weak, but is at home and up. He had a narrow escape. As for my car, well it is in the shop, and will cost $200.00 to get it in shape. I don't know yet what I can do about it. I haven't told Mama.

That's all,
DAD

"Bloody, but unbowed"

Friday
(May 14, 1937)

DEAR VERNON,

Good news! Mama is doing fine at home. Mrs. Conley came home yesterday and rested well last night. Harold is out and stirring around. My Chevrolet will be transferred to another hospital for treatment at a savings of $125. There the cost will be only $75, as against $200 at Johnson's. Everything O.K.

DAD

Tuesday
(May 18, 1937)

DEAR VERNON,

Mama continues to improve. She walked to dining room yesterday. She says she feels fine. Will remove bandages tomorrow.

Hope to get my car in a few days.

DAD

May 26, 1937

DEAR VERNON,

This afternoon I shall take your mother back to see Dr. Brenizer. Mrs. Conley will also go. I hope he will find them both in good shape. Mama went to the dining table for dinner yesterday, and in the evening I took her for a short ride to Roy Long's. The girl we have now, though young and inexperienced, is willing and fairly good as a cook. She is Doretha, Uncle Moze's kid, whom you may remember. I fired Madam Ernie, the $2.00 a day Negro, just as soon as I could go home when I found out her price. That was after six days. That was poor business, not to know what she charged—but I had to have help, and had tried so many places I was ready to pay any price for help.

Roger was initiated into the National Honor Society of High Schools this week. Sixteen of the 156 in Concord High who next year will be seniors, were tapped. Scholarship, character, service, and leadership are the points considered. It makes me proud of my little boy.

Roger has severe nose-bleeding spells. Dr. King advised me to see Dr. Rankin, nose specialist. Roger will see him today.

Harold has not been able to resume work yet. Dr. will take stitches from his severed tendons today.

Martha, I think, has made an unwise decision.

Mabel has been elected music teacher at Jonesboro.

I hope Miss White gets the place at Bonlee.

Affectionately,
DAD

June 1, '37

DEAR VERNON,

Last week on my way home after putting my boys to bed, I discovered a slight irritation on the convex surface of my rotund abdomen. "I have the heat," thought I. About nine o'clock it felt so uncomfortable that I went to the bathroom to powder the affected part. Pouring some talcum into my hand, I applied it the the surface made miserable by the "heat," and discovered that it had developed into a boil of curious shape. As my obesity prevented me from getting a view of the boil, I took down the mirror, and after some effort succeeded in getting a clear view of my afflicted stomach. What I beheld was a boil the size and shape of a fat grub worm, red as pokeberry juice, and in a scarlet field of sore flesh. By ten o'clock my boil had grown to the size and length of my finger. The surrounding area was flaming. That boil had turned into a rupture. Even then it seemed ready to burst through my delicate cuticle and ooze out on the bed. I got up and studied some literature I have on hospital insurance, but found that under the circumstance, I was too late. I looked at my receipt for burial insurance and rejoiced that it was paid, and that I was at last to reap some benefit from paid up insurance—no, I don't mean I rejoiced in that, but I felt it was so. I lay down and tried to hold my insides in with my hand, when I discovered that my rupture had changed to a cancer! I thought of screaming good-bye to Mama and the boys, when in my excitement my hand pressed heavily on my cancer. Then that blood blister which I had raised on my own stomach by my own strap while whipping the opposite side of a boy, burst. Gee, what a relief!

Mama continues to improve. She rode with me to Concord
Sat. night. Roger is the cook now. Does fine.

With love,
DAD

June 18, 1937

DEAR VERNON,

Tuesday passed without our customary letter from you. I hope
you are well and happy. Mama is feeling so much better.

Sunday Thelma and her husband, Mr. and Mrs. Liverman of
Charlotte, Margaret Liverman, and Miss Gilcott of Roxobel came
to see us.

DAD

July 26, 1937

DEAR VERNON,

After a very delightful vacation of one week, I am back in the
school-room. I left Mama at Sanford and took four other passengers from Cameron—Lula, Lillie Mae, and Nonnie Rogers
and Miss Mary Thomas. We visited Edenton, Elizabeth City, Kitty
Hawk, Nag's Head, Roanoke Island, Norfolk, Ocean View, and
Greenville. Cooked most of our meals on the way. With those
four women passengers I got lots of service and much waiting on.
We enjoyed every moment of it. If you can you should visit
Roanoke Island while the pageant is being given. It is very
impressive.

Mama tires out very easily, but I suppose is doing very well. It
will be some time before she regains her strength. I do wish she
could have gone with me. Yesterday was her birthday. Write.

DAD

August 10, 1937

DEAR VERNON,

> "Double, double,
> Toil and trouble,
> Fire burn
> And cauldron bubble."

Right merrily the cauldron of trouble doth bubble in our community. Many have added ingredients which are making a mess of a stew the like of which that concocted by the witches was savory. I have in the cauldron now one left leg containing red, inflamed varicose veins. And pain! And premonition of blood poison! And imagination. For fuel to keep the pot boiling I have contributed:

Loss of 1½ days work	$4.54
One doctors fee	2.00
One ace bandage	1.00
One rubber stocking	6.00
Medicine	2.00
Total cost of fuel	$15.54

My neighbors are making generous contributions to our community trouble spot too. Scot Summers put in three broken ribs. As fuel he contributed his father's new Oldsmobile. He was seeing if the new car would make 90. It did, but had to slow down when it began to go round and round and turn over and over. Scot is in the new Cabarrus Hospital.

Jeter Lee, teacher here, put in one bruised and battered body, and a scratched face. He gave his new Chevrolet as fuel. After coming from Miami—650 miles—in nine hours, he neared the city of Charlotte at 85 per. A tree stopped him. Damage $300.

G. D. Hudspeth, a neighbor boy who last year backed his dad's car over his baby brother killing him, turned his new Ford over Saturday, wrecking it badly.

Harold Ingraham, Mrs. Young's grandson, Elizabeth's son, is in hospital with diphtheria.

And so on and on.

Yes, I do remember Mrs. Penland. Give her and James my regards. I certainly would like to see them.

I stayed at Nags Head. Room cost me $1.50. I forget the lady's name but the place is a big wooden building on right of road, in which is housed the post office. I tried several places which were filled up. There are several places—hotels and rooming houses—on Roanoke Island, but they are usually well-filled they say. Nags Head is some eight miles away on the sandbanks.

If you have occasion to spend the night at Elizabeth City—a very interesting and a very friendly city, Eringhaus and Saunders to the contrary notwithstanding—please stop at the Iris Tourist Home and tell Mrs. Pritchett I have sent you to the *perfect house,* to a charming place to stay.

I also recommend Edenton. I could spend days there. The glory of the past is hers. See St. Pauls, the courthouse, the Teapot, the Cupola, Beverly Hall, the different mansions.

I gotta stop.

DAD

August 11, 1937

I stopped at Pleasant View Hotel—Mrs. M. C. Hollowell, proprietress. In plain view of ocean. Not elegant but comfortable enough. $1.50.

DAD

Nov. 4, 1937

DEAR VERNON,

This is the third letter I have written since July. I wonder if I have forgotten how? It is bad for a man to have a wife do all his writing for him, as he will soon feel like he just *can't* write.

I wish I could have seen Paul Green's play. It must be a stupendous production, judging from the number of characters. I enjoy things like that. If I had had the money I would have gone.

Last night the Oxford Orphanage singing class gave a performance at J.T.S. It was very good. I enjoyed seeing Cousin Walton Alderman again.

The road to Charlotte is closed for repairs. I want to go Saturday (to Charlotte) but will have to detour by old road, and it is very rough, they say. Want to take Mama back to see Dr. Brenizer. She doesn't seem to get strong.

Mrs. Conley returned to work the 1st. We are glad to have her back. She seems very well.

I have just received hospital insurance policies. I took it out for Mama, Roger, and myself. It is a good thing, I am sure.

Mildred seems to be making good use of her popularity at Mars Hill. I am glad.

We attended cottage prayer meeting in Concord at Mr. Lyttle's Tuesday night. It was conducted by Roger, and was an inspiration to us, and to all who attended. He is a very good speaker and is so earnest in his work.

October was a beautiful month. It was filled with unusual but pleasant events for me. Mr. Finley gave an oyster supper on the 7th to celebrate his and my birthday. One of my old boys who has been gone 12 years surprised me by giving me a Yellobole. Harold also gave me a Yellobole, so I now puff two good pipes. On the 8th a big barbecue was enjoyed at the school. On the 10th we attended a chicken and noodle supper at Kay Patterson's log cabin in Concord. I had lots of fun. Had not been to a party in 20 years.

Mrs. Garmon was buried Sunday. Mama and I attended funeral. Mr. Garmon is sick. Don't suppose he will last long.

My scribbling is terrible this A.M. I'm nervous. Maybe you can read it, but it looks like I had better let Mama do the writing.

DAD

Feb. 23, '38

DEAR VERNON,

It is so dark in my schoolroom this morning that I can hardly see to write. The rain is coming down in torrents. It is the first rain we have had in some time.

Mama went to see her doctor in Charlotte last week. He gave her some medicine, and I think it has helped her. Dr. Brenizer says she will not have to undergo another operation. I am so glad she will not have to go through that ordeal again. She seems much better.

Miss Greenlee will be confined to her room several weeks yet. She went to see her doctor Monday. He says she will be able to see, but that she must be very careful for a month yet and not try to even walk without help. Mama is staying with her today.

My cold hangs on. I had flu and was out for 5½ days, and I just don't seem able to get rid of the after effects.

I sent the letter you wrote for me about the talking book, but have had no reply. It has been more than a month since I sent it off.

We certainly enjoy the radio. Now that things are as they are in Europe, we are eager to hear the news broadcasts from London and Berlin. The reception is splendid.

I hope you will be able to sell all the blocks you can make. How many will the machine turn out per day? Will the blocks be much more expensive than brick?

John Russell has high blood pressure and has to lie about for ten or fifteen days. He has not worked now in a week.

Mrs. Conley is matron at Indian Cottage.

Affectionately,
DAD

April 21, 1938

DEAR VERNON,

It is cool and rainy this morning. In fact it is so cold a fire would feel good. If it does not soon turn warmer I shall have to buy some more coal. Wintertime is such an expensive time to live. My coal bill has been high this winter, I just must begin trying to save a little each month to send Roger to college. I owe only $8.50 more on my wicked car, and $45 to Mrs. Conley—a part of the money I borrowed to pay hospital bills. Harold hasn't paid his hospital expenses which I paid for him. However, I hope to have everything paid up in a few months. If Roger can get work when school is out, maybe he can make enough to buy his clothes and a typewriter. Elroy has no work.

Don't suppose I will have any vacation this year as I have already taken up all my time while sick. But I do want to go down to see your Aunt Laura some weekend. I had a letter from Lucille last week and she said Laura has not been at all well for some time, and wants to see me. She is 70 years old, I think.

Your mother enjoyed her trip to the Thomases last week. She went with a Houston boy and Harold. It was cheap trip for her, costing only 80¢.

Mr. Fisher is in hospital in Charlotte. Appendix operation. Since he is away, I don't suppose we will have a show tonight, as no one else here can operate the machine. I don't care much, as the order and the odor in the auditorium are not so good. I would like to see *Lost Horizon* if it comes to Concord. We haven't been to a show in more than a year—except at J.T.S.

Haden Talbert has bought the lot in front of our house. Don't know whether he will build on it or not.

Have you made any blocks yet?

I wrote Uncle Ike Monday. Hope he can soon be at home.

With love,

DAD

Johnson said he certainly appreciated your letter.

June 10, 1938

DEAR VERNON,

Last night I just could not go to sleep until after two o'clock. But shortly after two a shower of rain descended in torrents, and it lulled me off to sleep. This morning is beautiful.

It was a real pleasure we had last night to see Shirley Temple in *The Stowaway*. Although it was so hot and odoriferous in the auditorium, I forgot that in my enjoyment of the play.

Work on our new gymnasium and hospital is progressing rapidly. The hospital is in the yard back of my cottage. It has messed up our playground.

How do you like your new car? What kind is it? I have had a little work done on mine, and it needs some more which I will have done next month, maybe.

Are you still making some good blocks? I went back one evening late to the block plant near Kannapolis but there was no one there. It was Saturday and they were not working.

I have a day and a half for vacation this year. It will begin July 4, and end the next day at noon. I had planned to take a week, but due to the fact that I am going to send Roger to Mars Hill this fall, I can't lose the time. And, too, Mama says she is not able to take much of a trip anywhere. However, I plan to go to see Laura.

With love,
DAD

Sept. 6, 1938
(Sevierville, Tenn.)

Having a glorious time.[1]

DAD

Friday
(Sept. 10, 1938)

We got home yesterday at three P.M. after a very fine trip. The weather was nice and cool, a few showers, and the scenery was wonderful. No bad luck except I had to buy a new battery at Newport, Tenn. Mama got along fine and enjoyed the trip. Haven't heard from Roger. Think he will like it all right. He rooms in private home.

DAD

(Sept. 16, 1938)

DEAR VERNON,

I am at work again after a very delightful vacation. We never enjoyed a trip any more than we did this one. Mama was very well and was as ready for adventure as I. Scenery in the Smoky Mountains is grand.

I hope your blocks will harden yet. Have you tried spreading sacks or cloths over them and keep them dampened? I notice they do that at the plant here.

Roger is getting plenty of work. Seems to like Mars Hill.

DAD

Nov. 2, 1938

DEAR VERNON,

I am returning the $6.00 I borrowed from you when you were

---

[1]Having taken Roger to enter Mars Hill College, Will and Blanche spent a few days in the mountains of North Carolina and Tennessee.

140

at home. Thank you for the loan even though I did not get the shed since we sold the cow. We hated to part with "Cynda," but Mama was not able to tend to her, and Elroy just couldn't milk. He tried and tried but failed to extract enough lacteal fluid to use on a saucer of cereal.

Mama attended the funeral yesterday of Mildred Helms. She was taken sick Sunday morning, and passed away in the evening. Spurgeon did not get home until after she was gone. She was seventeen.

Roger has moved into much better quarters. He now has steam heat, and is in the same house with Spurgeon Helms and Ivan Kizer. He likes it much better.

Mama, Mrs. Conley, Miss Greenlee, Mrs. Harris, and I went to Charlotte Sunday to hear the gospel singer, Edward MacHugh. We enjoyed it very much. The crowd was dense. Several thousand—it is stated—were not able to get in the church where he sang.

Elsie and Murlie Asbell spent the week end with us and Myrtle. I like Murlie fine. She calls us Uncle Will and Aunt Blanche.

Thursday night Dr. I. G. Greer, of the Mills Home, is to give a Folk Song recital and lecture at Hotel Concord. He will be accompanied by his wife who will play the dulcimer—whatever that is. We plan to go.

We will be mighty glad for you to bring Aunt Sallie. Let us know a few days beforehand so we can make things comfortable for her.

With love,
DAD

November 16, 1938

DEAR VERNON,

We were glad to receive letters from you, Harold, and Roger yesterday. Harold had no news except that his pants were worn out. Roger's letter was full of the happenings at Mars Hill written in his usual sincere style. He is mighty glad Dr. Moore has returned from Johns Hopkins after having had a serious operation.

We received Roger's report last week. It was tops on every one of his five subjects.

How many rooms do you plan to have in your house? Roger might like to work for you during vacation. I do hope he can work somewhere. Did you design the proposed house yourself?

Aunt Laura has been right sick, but is better now. She had Lucille to write for me to come to see her, but I could not get off last week. Unless she gets worse I will not go now.

If Mama is able she and I are to be Mrs. Conley's guests at the food show in Charlotte tonight. But since Mama has been "poorly" for several days we may not go.

With love,

DAD